OVERCOMING HOMOSEXUALITY

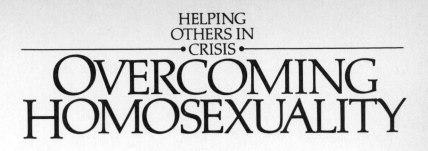

HELPING
OTHERS IN
• CRISIS •

OVERCOMING HOMOSEXUALITY

ED HURST
WITH DAVE AND NETA
JACKSON

David C. Cook Publishing Co.
Elgin, Illinois—Weston, Ontario

David C. Cook Publishing Co.
Elgin, Illinois—Weston, Ontario
Overcoming Homosexuality
© 1987 by Ed Hurst and Dave and Neta Jackson

92 91 90 89   5   4   3   2

Scripture quotations, unless otherwise noted, are from the *Holy Bible: New International Version* © 1978 by the New York International Bible Society. Used by permission of Zondervan Bible Publishers.

The photographs contained on the cover and throughout this book are staged dramatizations and are for illustrative purposes only. These photographs do not depict actual persons engaged in the situations described in this book, nor are they intended to do so.

Published by David C. Cook Publishing Co.
850 N. Grove Ave., Elgin, IL 60120
Cable address: DCCOOK
Designed by Christopher Patchel
Photo by Jim Whitmer
Illustrated by Jane Sterrett
Printed in the United States of America
Library of Congress Catalog Number: 86-72964

ISBN: 1-55513-824-1

Homosexual offenders . . .
That is what some of you were.
But you were washed,
you were sanctified,
you were justified
in the name of the Lord Jesus Christ
and by the Spirit of our God.
—I Corinthians 6:9, 11

Contents

Preface

WHEN WE WERE FIRST INVITED TO WORK ON THIS BOOK with Ed Hurst, we felt honored. In our years of pastoral ministry, we had encountered people who struggled with homosexual tendencies. As we prayed for and ministered to these people, we often wished for materials to help us better serve them.

In this book Ed Hurst has provided a tool we wish we had had years ago. No, it won't provide every answer. No, it doesn't contain a quick cure. No, it is not a psychology text. It is, quite simply, a Christian workers resource book. With the wealth of material it contains, you can lead others toward a Christ-centered life-style, and away from the homosexual life-style.

Ed Hurst left his homosexual life-style over 12 years ago. He has over ten years of experience counseling others who struggle with the problem, and he has been honest enough to acknowledge his own ongoing struggles. This book contains his opinions, some that other Christians may differ on. In this book, he shares what he has learned and lived in this difficult job of "Helping Others in Crisis."

Ed has taken the time to do the thinking and Biblical and clinical study necessary to identify the origins of homosexuality and thereby the factors leading to freedom. His conclusions are being confirmed by the work of some of the best Christian researchers in the field. He doesn't offer a magic solution that claims instant freedom from all inclinations and temptations, but he has had steady fruit in his own life and in the lives of those he counsels as they continue to experience greater strength and freedom.

There still remain those (even some Christians) who claim that change is impossible. And yet they are confounded by the work of Ed and others connected with networks all across the country like EXODUS International. Every person who does change proves those gloomy claims false and gives hope to others who would like to change.—Dave and Neta Jackson

THE POTENTIAL FOR CHANGE: MY TESTIMONY

WHEN I MADE A DECISION TO FOLLOW THE LORD IN 1974, I had never heard of anyone overcoming homosexuality. This disturbed me greatly. My other sins—drinking, smoking, taking drugs, lying, etc.—were all things that I *did*, but homosexuality was different; it described who I was. No other facet of my life equaled homosexuality in prominence. It had been with me for as long as I could remember.

My mother relates that I was different from the time I was an infant. As I grew older, those differences continued. Throughout my elementary school years I was always on the fringe, never really one of the gang.

In my neighborhood, I frequently preferred to play more domestic games like ''school'' and ''house'' instead of games like ''war'' and ''jailbreak.''

During my early teen years, my perfectionism and sense of ethics earned me the nicknames of ''Mr. Dictionary'' and ''Mr. Rulebook.'' Even though I had a bunch of guys that I hung out with, I still never truly fit in.

With the onset of puberty I began to realize even more of the differences between myself and others. While other guys began to develop a fascination in the obvious physical development of the girls in our class, I was preoccupied with the development of other guys. I pursued adolescent experimentation with scientific curiosity. Others were experimenting, too. But somehow I sensed that for them it was just a phase. For me, however, I concluded that the reason I was looking at boys was because I was gay. Then I decided that I wasn't gay because I was different, but I was different because I was gay. All of this took place between ages 11 and 13.

Throughout my adolescence, I ''studied'' homosexuality. The books that I found portrayed it as an unfortunate, unchangeable malady. Many of them characterized homosexuals as dark and sinister people—degenerates and perverts. I could not identify

7

with these images. I was only searching for love and fulfillment. What was so dark and sinister about that? In many ways, I was more moral than my straight counterparts who continually boasted of their sexual conquests. My romantic dream was to save myself for marriage—to another man.

This dream even played into my first experience with the Lord. I had been in love with a young man for over a year. He was actually straight, and had told me our friendship couldn't go anywhere physically. Up until this point I had not embarked on an adult homosexual life-style, even though I considered myself gay. But I hung in there as a determined, faithful suitor, romantically dreaming that it would somehow work out.

Then he called me one day to tell me of his conversion. Jealous of this One who was meeting my friend's needs, I attended the next prayer meeting to see what was happening. It was there that I had my first sense that both God and Jesus were real. Unfortunately, my friend fell away within two weeks.

Shortly thereafter, some of the Christians in the group began telling me that I had to give up one of my other friends (who was gay) because he was an evil person. I couldn't understand that— at least not the way they put it. This other friend seemed just like me. I had known him for years. I couldn't understand how they could be compassionate toward me and regard him as the hated enemy. That became the excuse I used to walk away from the Lord.

That was in 1970. And I told the Lord, "You are a crutch; I don't want a crutch; I don't need a crutch. If You are real, come back when I'm on top."

About nine months later I went off to college. At college, I had my first "coming out" homosexual experience as an adult. From that point on, I began hanging out with the gays on campus. At first I didn't have sex that frequently, because I was always looking for a special person. But the frequency and then the variety of partners began to increase over the years. Later I made efforts to start a gay-lib organization on campus and even let my family know.

Finally, I moved into the city and got an apartment and pursued the bar scene.

The summer of 1974 found me on top of the world. I had made my place in the gay community. I had lots of friends, a good job, and a fun life. I could afford to get high when I wanted, and yet it wasn't interfering with my work. Furthermore, I had met the guy of my dreams. We planned to quit the bar scene, "get married," and set up house together. Everything seemed to be working out.

I was sitting at the gay bar one night, waiting for my lover to meet me, when I looked up and noticed a guy heading for the dance floor preening and primping and putting everything together. All of a sudden it struck me that I was in a "meat market," and I wasn't going to find love there.

It was then that the Lord spoke to me and said, "That's right, son. You're on top now, but you can see that it's empty. Why don't you come back to Me?"

I was so shocked at how the Lord had done what I had asked four years before that I left the bar telling some friends that when my lover showed up to tell him that I wasn't coming back. In the lining of an old "bomber" jacket, I found some tracts that some street evangelists had given me some time in the past. They became my first Bible as I gave my life to Jesus.

I don't know what people thought that week when I walked into church. My blond hair, bleached a brassy gold, was long and curly; my voice was cultivated to be high pitched and girlish, and my face was soft, fair, and quite feminine. I had a long way to go. (It is important to realize that I happened to fit the stereotype image of a gay—most do not.)

In the years that have transpired since then, I have learned much about the character and nature of God. I have learned much about His ability to transform and renew individuals. I have also learned much about the true nature of homosexuality, not only as it applied to my own life but also to the lives of hundreds of others.

In 1976, when I went off to Bible school, my primary motivation was to learn enough about the Bible to find answers for my own homosexual struggles. Within several months after my arrival, however, other struggling students began coming to me for help and counsel. Reluctantly, I began to counsel and to head up a street ministry to gays. The following summer I attended the second annual conference of EXODUS held in Oakland, California. EXODUS is a national network of evangelical, Christian ministries that believe homosexuality is reversible. At this conference I met other individuals from around the United States who had come out of a gay background and were in some form of active ministry to other homosexuals. I also met Robbi Kenney, the founder of OUTPOST, one of the oldest ex-gay ministries in the country.

She was looking for a man "with a testimony" to help her run the OUTPOST ministry; I joined her in 1978.

In 1979 I presented my testimony at CAPS, the Christian Association for Psychological Studies. While there, Robbi Kenney and I also participated in a debate with delegates who did *not* believe change was possible. Most prominent of these was Dr. Ralph Blair, founder and head of Evangelicals Concerned.

In a private conversation, Blair was quite surprised when I admitted that I still had homosexual temptations. He told me that I was the first ex-gay he had met to admit that. Both privately and publicly, I admitted to those temptations but also to the fact that those temptations were diminishing in both frequency and intensity. I challenged conference participants to find a Biblical definition of change that included the *absence of temptation*. The temptation to fornicate does not make one a fornicator. Why, then, should homosexual temptations make one a homosexual?

But these discussions with Blair and others in the pro-gay movement (which tries to justify homosexuality on the basis that "it's the way God made some people, and it can't be changed") challenged me to find the causes of homosexuality. If a person was not born a homosexual, then what happened to make him or her one? And could that condition be truly reversed? *I* was personally finding increased freedom, but why and how? Others, who were valiantly remaining ex-gay, seemed to be doing it only by guilt and grit. They seemed to hope for nothing more than the grace to *endure* a life of celibacy. I was convinced God offered more than that.

My research led to an understanding of certain causes or "roots of homosexuality," as I've come to call them. Homosexuality, I am convinced, is the manifestation of certain emotional dynamics that combine to create an initial homosexual identity. To address homosexuality alone is to attempt to cap a volcano. The fire still burns. I believe, however, that the fire can be put out. Homosexuality is curable. In time, even the homosexual fantasies and desires and temptations can diminish. I, and many other counselors, have used this approach very effectively for more than six years.

What has been the fruit? It is difficult to arrive at "follow-up" statistics. Many individuals who come for counseling terminate when they feel they have the problem under control. While we'd like to assume that all of these have made it, that is most likely not the case.

I feel safe in saying that of the 100-plus homosexual individuals whom I have had some part in counseling, at least 50% of them are making it. Of those who began with a sincere commitment and motivation to change, at least 80% are making it. Another 10% are struggling but still fighting, and another 10% are losing or have lost hope. This is a subjective opinion without statistical back-up since this is not an easy area to "document."

Currently, I know several hundred former gays in various stages of recovery. A number of these are ministry leaders in the EXODUS network.

It has now been more than a dozen years since I first committed myself to follow the Lord. In those years, I have not fallen sexually with another man, although I have had struggles with temptation, fantasy, and pornography. Even though I am still single, I do not regard my single state as a by-product of my homosexual struggles. I know many former homosexuals who are now married—some happily, others not. Like most singles, I anticipate marriage and continue dating with that end in mind.—Ed Hurst

CHAPTER ONE

WHAT IS THE
CURRENT SITUATION?

T HERE IS NO QUESTION THAT HOMOSEXUALITY HAS "COME out of the closet" in recent years. Newspapers abound in stories about gay rights, the AIDS epidemic, child-custody cases, church-ordination conflicts, and renowned individuals who have admitted (or announced) their homosexuality. "Dear Abby" and Ann Landers address homosexual questions regularly. "Dr. Ruth" and Phil Donahue almost make it seem commonplace. Popular movies have brought it to mass attention.

Psychological Views

Many of the psychology professions accept homosexuality as normal and consider the segments of society that oppose it as intolerant. It is now considered "unethical" for a licensed psychologist to call it either a problem or a disorder. A new term, "ego-dystonic homosexuality," was created to accommodate those clients who view their homosexuality as a "problem." That category has recently been eliminated.

To justify such a drastic change in attitude, one would expect that some major breakthroughs in the understanding of homosexuality had occurred. Theories do abound; however, a review of the literature over the last 20 years does not reveal any significant findings showing homosexuality to be an inborn characteristic. Dr. Robert Kronemeyer, a medical doctor with over a quarter of a century of clinical experience treating people who struggle with homosexuality, categorically states, "With rare exceptions, homosexuality is neither inherited nor the result of some glandular disturbance or the scrambling of genes or chromosomes. Homosexuals are made, not born 'that way.' From my 25 years' experience as a clinical psychologist, I firmly believe that homosexuality is a *learned* response to early painful experiences and that it can be *unlearned*."[1]

Statistics

No reliable statistics are available to accurately detail either how many homosexuals currently exist or if their numbers are growing. However, many researchers do accept a ten percent figure. It has been impossible to obtain a random sample of American homosexual men and women. Many would be unlikely—now or in the future—to participate in such a research study.

I believe that many groups (whether they are gay political groups or Christian action groups) determine the size of either their local or the national gay population subjectively according to how they believe their "environment" fits the statistic. The average percent from which most organizations add or subtract is ten percent.

In my opinion, the numbers probably are growing. Perhaps the growing tolerance for homosexuality will enable many who might not have gotten involved previously to now engage in the practices of the homosexual life-style. I believe that the breakdown of the family and the widespread effects of the media have also added to the numbers. One other factor may be that adolescent individuals who think they *might* be gay are no longer being discouraged from assuming a homosexual identity but are being encouraged from many quarters to develop that identity.

How are these statistics relevant to your church? Start with the possibility of a 10% homosexual community. It is conceivable that 40% of our general population deals with this problem on an intimate level—assuming an average of two parents and one other family member for each of the one-in-ten people who are personally homosexual. It is possible that many of our church groups have within them people who need help—people for whom homosexuality is a personal crisis. I recall when my testimony, "Once Gay, Always Gay?" appeared in the September 4, 1978, issue of *Christian Life* magazine. One pastor of a small church in a town of just a few thousand people wrote to the editor protesting, "Why is it necessary to speak of this 'unspeakable' sin when it is a problem that most pastors will never have to deal with?"

When I read his name and the town where he had pastored, I marveled at the timing. This man pastored in *my* hometown, just ten blocks from where I lived! I knew the families who lived on either side of his church, and a former pastor in that church had rented the house directly across the street from me. Yes, it is very possible that people in your church are hurting because a friend or relative is involved in a homosexual relationship, or they themselves are struggling with homosexuality. I hope this book will be a help to you in recognizing and helping these hurting people.

An open homosexual life-style thrives more easily in larger cities. Most cities have at least one gay bar and a "cruising" district, a park or street where homosexuals come to meet and pick up willing partners. In some cities, the majority of homosexual activities take place at rest stops or truck stops or in locally known rest rooms. While some recruiting may go on in these places, most homosexuals, are only interested in willing partners. Many would prefer a bar or a "more normal" meeting place, but for some in smaller communities, these public places are the only options available.

Patterns

Usually, homosexual men (generally called *gays*) and homosexual women (*lesbians*) don't mix—they have little in common except their distinction from heterosexuals. Most gay bars have a high percentage of males and few, if any, lesbians. Men are more prone to one-night stands while women, for the most part, are looking for relationships. For men, it may be safe to say that the bar is a primary place for meeting new sexual partners; women tend to develop their relationships in less "intentional" environments. Part of this may be due to our society's basic standards for same-sex behavior. Women are permitted to be more physically intimate in public than men. Likewise, close and intimate relationships between women are not viewed as suspiciously as the same kind of relationships between men.

It is my personal opinion that there are more gay men than lesbian women. Of course, this is difficult to prove, but I believe that peer pressure and identity conflicts contribute greatly to the development of a homosexual identity. These conflicts seem to victimize white males more than any other group. There is more pressure to "prove your manhood" than to "prove your womanhood." Our standards for maleness are more rigid than our standards for femaleness. Failure to live up to these rigid standards can lead to despair of making it in the straight world and an acceptance of a homosexual identity.

Stereotype Images

The homosexual culture is full of diversity. The typical image of a homosexual is an exaggerated stereotype. The limp wrists, lisp, swaying hips, and flamboyant clothing are not very popular in the gay culture today. While some homosexuals adopt these affectations for identification purposes, they are not indicative of mainstream gay culture. Homosexual males can be ruggedly masculine. Many, particularly in the younger set, prefer jeans to flashier clothing. They come from many differing vocations. While a high percentage of males in the theater, the arts, or hair design might be gay, these represent only a fraction of the homosexual culture. I believe it is safe to say that while many of us can recognize some homosexuals most of the time, none of us can recognize all of them all of the time.

The same holds true for lesbians. The truck driver or motorcycle riding images are basically stereotypes. While some do fit those images, many are more typically feminine in appearance. There is no surefire way to pick one out in a crowd.

Terminology

Sometimes the words "gay" and "homosexual" are used to describe both men and women. This is acceptable unless a distinction is being made. Then the preferred terms are "gay" and "lesbian." Many Christians detest the word "gay" and refuse to use it, saying that homosexuality is anything but gay. Homosexuals' happiness is not true happiness as it would be known in a committed walk with the Lord, but *they* don't have any experience for knowing that. And they may not believe that you know enough about homosexuality to make the contrast for them. To them, they have most likely known years of confusion, rejection, and oppression. The gay life-style and the gay relationships provide for many their first sense of identity, acceptance, security, and the promise of sexual fulfillment.

Be careful of the terms you use in a ministry to homosexuals. Some may cause alienation. If we want to help these people, they may reject our help if we use these words—for example: "homo," "sodomite," and "pervert"—even if they are Biblical words.

CHAPTER TWO

THE BIBLICAL WITNESS

F OR A LONG TIME THERE WAS VERY LITTLE QUESTION AS TO what Scripture said about homosexual behavior. Nine books in the Bible (six in the Old Testament and three in the New) offer clear-cut indications that it greatly displeased God. This, of course, didn't mean that there weren't Christians who struggled with or even practiced homosexuality, but they didn't try to offer any theological justification for overt practice.

But for the last 30 years, liberal persons have challenged the traditional and most obvious understanding of these texts. Some of these people aren't advocating promiscuous homosexuality. What they claim is that homosexual "marriages" between mature, loving, and faithful partners are as Biblically acceptable as good heterosexual marriages. I believe they are wrong.

IN THE BEGINNING

Before looking at the specific texts that speak about homosexuality, let me set the stage concerning God's intention for marriage, since that is what gay theologians claim to achieve.

In the Creation accounts of Genesis 1 and 2 there are three things about marriage relevant to the issue of homosexuality.

1. *"Male and female he created them"* (Gen. 1:27). It's conceivable that God could have gotten by with only one sex in His creation of humans. He demonstrated in lower forms of life several viable designs for unisex procreation. And today's science fiction authors have thought of other models. But God didn't take that route. He designed humans as male and female.

Psychiatrist Erik Erikson identifies *generativity,* pouring our life back into future generations, as adults' most meaningful function. And that occurs most profoundly in procreation. There, in an ongoing way, we function "in the image of God" by participating in His act of Creation. But this participation is restricted through Creation itself to the union of the two sexes. This fact lends new insight to verse 27: "So God created man in his own image, in the image of God he created him; male and female he created them.''

2. *One becomes two to become one.* In discussing the method by which Genesis 2 reports that God created two sexes, John R. W. Stott suggests that there was very specific consequence and meaning in woman being created out of man. It resulted in man no longer being complete in his own sex.

He says, ''Even the inattentive reader will be struck by the three references to 'flesh': 'this is . . . flesh of my flesh . . . they will become one flesh.'

''We may be certain that this is deliberate, not accidental. It teaches that heterosexual intercourse in marriage is more than a union; it is a kind of reunion. It is not a union of alien persons who do not belong to one another and cannot appropriately become one flesh. On the contrary, it is the union of two persons who originally were one, were then separated from each other, and now in the sexual encounter of marriage come together again.

''It is surely this that explains the profound mystery of heterosexual intimacy.''[1]

And it is interesting to note that in many ways even homosexuals acknowledge the depth of this heterosexual mystery by not behaving as the same *(homo)* sex they claim to be. They frequently *emulate* two sexes, contriving in a variety of ways to be the counterparts to one another that all humans need—one more assertive and the other receptive, one more ''masculine'' and the other more ''feminine.'' You may be surprised to discover that the third most common sexual fantasy for male and female homosexuals is *heterosexual* in nature.

3. *Marriage requires ''a man'' and ''his wife.''* There was only one aspect of the initial events of creation that was ''not good.'' God said, ''It is not good for the man to be alone. I will make a helper suitable for him'' (Gen. 2:18). God then parades all the animals before Adam, ''But for Adam no suitable helper was found'' (vs. 20). I believe that it is legitimate to understand this as more than the animals. It was a consideration of *all* the options. Even the daily communion with God had not satiated man's aloneness. A totally new creation was required.

After Adam notes the mystery of Eve's being taken out of him, the Scripture says, ''For this reason a man will leave his father and mother and be united to his wife, and they will

18

become one flesh'' (Gen. 2:24). This was God's provision for man's aloneness. It is the only provision acknowledged as marriage in the whole Bible.

Jesus affirmed it exactly: "But at the beginning of creation God 'made them male and female.' 'For this reason a man . . .' " etc. (Mk. 10:6-8). Then Jesus says, "Therefore what God has joined together, let man not separate" (vs. 9). This, of course, refers to any specific marriage, but by implication also applies to the *institution* of marriage—what God has set up, let man not alter.

The only time when marriage between a man and a woman is not spoken of as ideal is when Paul, who was single and expecting persecution, says, "I wish that all men were as I am. But each man has his own gift from God; one has this gift; another has that" (I Cor. 7:7). Certainly God does give a gift of celibacy to some; for those not called to celibacy but not yet married, Scripture requires the *discipline* of sexual abstinence. While the Bible acknowledges that discipline of any kind is difficult, it is not viewed as onerous. On the contrary, it has many beneficial by-products. But the only other Biblical option to the discipline of sexual abstinence is marriage between a man and a woman.

THE BIBLE AND HOMOSEXUAL BEHAVIOR

The nine books of the Bible that deal with homosexual behavior fit into four categories: (1) the two narratives of the cities of Sodom and Gibeah, (2) prohibitions in the Mosaic Law and violation thereof, (3) the Romans 1 label of "perversion," and (4) the inclusion of homosexual behavior in lists of sins.

1. Sodom and Gibeah

There are two incidents reported of similar nature (though hundreds of years apart) involving homosexual behavior. The first is found in Genesis 18:20—19:25 about the city of Sodom, from which the word *sodomy* is derived. The Lord sent two angels to Sodom to discover, as it were, whether the sin of that city (and also Gomorrah) was as severe as had been reported. Lot, who lived in Sodom, met them at the gate and insisted that they stay with him rather than in the city square where they intended to stay. However, "before they had gone to bed, all the men from every part of the city of Sodom—both young and old—surrounded the house. They called to Lot, 'Where are the men who came to you tonight? Bring them out to us so that we can have sex with *[yada]* them.'

"Lot went outside to meet them and shut the door behind him and said, 'No, my friends. Don't do this wicked thing. Look, I have two daughters who have never slept with [*yada*] a man. Let me bring them out to you, and you can do what you like with them. But don't do anything to these men, for they have come under the protection of my roof'" (Gen. 19:4-8).

The men of Sodom refused the offer, berated Lot for presuming to judge them (calling their intentions a wicked thing), threatened to do worse with Lot than with his guests, and then they attempted to break the door down. The angels blinded the men of Sodom and pulled Lot back in to safety. Then the angels warned Lot and his family to flee the city before they destroyed it.

Some pro-gay advocates attempt to reinterpret this rather forthright story by claiming that the Hebrew word, *yada*, translated in the above New International Version as "have sex with" and in the King James and other versions as "know," should not be taken sexually. The word occurs 943 times in the Old Testament, and only ten explicitly mean sexual intercourse. Therefore, they suggest we translate the phrase: "so that we may get acquainted with them;" possibly their "credentials" as foreigners needed examining. As support for this view they offer the fact that other Old Testament references to the sin of Sodom (Ezekiel 16:49, 50 and Jeremiah 23:14) do not mention homosexuality as the wickedness that brought on the city's destruction, and indeed it wasn't the only sin.

There are three major flaws in this argument.

First, translation by majority rule would result in the minority meanings of words never coming through. Context must be the primary consideration. For instance, one of the sexually explicit uses of the word *yada* occurs in Genesis 4:25, "And Adam knew *[yada]* his wife again; and she bare a son" (KJV). If one were to use majority rule, one could say something like, "Adam got acquainted with his wife again, and she had a son."

Second, *this* context demands a sexual understanding. Lot's offer of his virgin daughters to appease the men is unquestionably a sexual offer. Why else would Lot offer such a tragic sacrifice if the men's intentions weren't overtly sexual? If all the men of Sodom wanted was to get acquainted, why not invite them in for a "cup of coffee"? If it was to interrogate the strangers, why not cooperate or buy them off with a financial bribe? (Lot was living in this valley because of the available wealth.) Lot's offer of a sexual bribe to deter them from doing what he calls a "wicked thing" demands a textual conclusion that their intention was somehow in line with his offer—sexual. Also, the threat to Lot by the men of the city, "We'll treat you *worse* than them," proves beyond question that their intentions weren't a simple breach of hospitality.

Third, Jude 7 explicitly identifies the wickedness in question as sexual: "In a similar way, Sodom and Gomorrah and the surrounding towns gave themselves up to sexual immorality and perversion." It is claimed by some pro-gays that by New Testament times *tradition* had caused this interpretation of Sodom's sin, therefore, it can't be trusted. But we cannot dismiss the commentary of one portion of Scripture on another as being corrupted by tradition without doing unacceptable damage to a faithful understanding of inspiration.

(II Peter 2:6-10 also refers to the practices in Sodom and Gomorrah as "filthy" and "lawless"; however, they are not explicitly identified as sexual in nature.)

A similar story occurs in Judges 19:22-27. An old man of the city of Gibeah invited a sojourning Levite, his servant, and his concubine to stay in his home for the night. But after dinner some wicked men of the city demanded: "Bring out the man who came to your house so we can have sex with [*yada*] him" (vs. 22). The homeowner refused but finally offered his virgin daughter and the Levite's concubine. The men of the city raped [*yada*] the concubine and abused her throughout the night before dumping her dead on the householder's doorstep. The incident led to war between the Israelites and the Benjamites who were defending Gibeah, and a terrible slaughter ensued.

Again, some want to reinterpret this story. They suggest that the "wicked men" "pounding on the door" intent on doing a "vile" and "disgraceful" deed—as Scripture describes the event—were only wanting to *know* the Levite in some nonsexual way.

These explanations outreach many people's credulity. David Field, author of *The Homosexual Way: A Christian Option?*, says, "In both passages this view involves taking the word *know*

21

in completely different senses in the space of four verses (meaning 'to become acquainted' in Gen. 19:5 and Jdg. 19:22 but clearly 'to have intercourse with' in Gen. 19:8 and Jdg. 19:25).''[2]

A more reasonable argument by gay theologians is that these stories, if they are about sexual demands, would be no more acceptable if the targets of the threatened assaults had been heterosexual. They would attribute the wickedness in both instances to gang rape, and no responsible gay person advocates that. But there are other passages relevant to the homosexual question.

2. The Mosaic Law and Its Violations

As the Children of Israel left Egypt, God began teaching them about Himself and His ways. There were the existential lessons from His daily guidance, protection, and provision in the wilderness. And there was the Law given on Mt. Sinai. They were leaving the wickedness of Egypt, but God knew that His people would be going back into the land where the same culture thrived that Lot had encountered in Sodom.

As with the cities of Sodom and Gomorrah, which God felt had to be utterly destroyed, so, too, had the people in the entire country become so wicked that they had to be eliminated. Later, when the Israelites entered the land, God issued startling instructions about how, in certain cases, almost nothing of the culture, the people, or even their animals was to be preserved. And yet, even in the process of conquest, He knew His people would be exposed to, and potentially influenced in a very negative way by, the culture of Canaan.

After issuing numerous sanitary and ceremonial laws, God turns to the specific issue of sexual relations: "I am the Lord your God. You must not do as they do in Egypt, where you used to live, and you must not do as they do in the land of Canaan, where I am bringing you. Do not follow their practices" (Lev. 18:1-3). Then, after prohibiting incest, adultery, and infanticide, God says the following:

Do not lie with a man as one lies with a woman; that is detestable.

Do not have sexual relations with an animal and defile yourself with it. A woman must not present herself to an animal to have sexual relations with it; that is a perversion.

Do not defile yourselves in any of these ways, because this is how the nations that I am going to drive out before you became defiled (Lev. 18:22-24).

Two chapters later the punishments for these sins are detailed.

If a man lies with a man as one lies with a woman, both of them have done what is detestable. They must be put to death; their blood will be on their own heads (Lev. 20:13).

In Deuteronomy the subject of homosexuality in the form of male temple prostitutes (and female prostitutes) is also addressed.

No Israelite man or woman is to become a shrine prostitute. You must not bring the earnings of a female prostitute or of a male prostitute into the house of the Lord your God to pay any vow, because the Lord your God detests them both (Deut. 23:17, 18).

Some gay theologians have suggested that the only concern of the Mosaic Law was the idolatrous nature of the pagan religions. They point out that racially mixed marriages were also prohibited with the clear reason being the danger of importing foreign religious loyalties into the nation. That may be reasonable if we had only the law in Deuteronomy. And yet taken together, these instructions seem to cover *both* personal homosexual behavior as well as the institutionalized form connected with religious idolatry. The passages in Leviticus seem to have to do with personal, practical living and are sandwiched among prohibitions on bestiality, incest, and adultery, which most gay theologians do not attempt to justify. A similar objection has been that these prohibitions are part of the "Holiness Code," and if one is to take literally these condemnations, then why not observe all the other aspects of the Code such as prohibitions on eating lobsters, rare steak, rabbit, etc.? And what about the penalty? Should one advocate the death penalty for homosexual behavior?

To the first point, it is a mistake to confuse dietary laws that have been repealed in the New Testament (Acts 10:9-16) with moral prohibitions that are reaffirmed in the New Testament (I Cor. 6:9-11 and I Tim. 1:10). What parts of the Law are relevant for Christians and which are obsolete may fall on a spectrum requiring interpretation where the New Testament is silent but not where the New Testament speaks.

As to the practice of the death penalty, it has already been served in Christ. But the fact that the Gospel offers pardon and forgiveness does not justify further sin. Jesus dealt with the woman caught in adultery by blocking the death penalty and forgiving her. But He also said, "Go now and leave your life of sin" (Jn. 8:11). Kenneth Gangel, president of Miami Christian College, says, "It is not a question of punishment, but rather a question of confession, i.e., the admission of homosexuality as sin, that is at the crux of the whole problem."[3]

The Israelites' violation of the Law in the matter of homosexuality is recorded on a personal level in the story of Gibeah and in the area of idolatry in several instances. The evil kings of Israel and Judah introduced male prostitutes into the land and the good kings who followed set themselves to purge the land of these practices (I Kings 14:24; 15:12; 22:46; II Kings 23:4-8). Of course, the introduction of male shrine prostitutes was not the only idolatrous thing promoted by the evil kings. Other practices were also borrowed from the Canaanites.

3. Romans 1 and 'Perversion'

Both Jesus and Peter, speaking from a primarily Jewish perspective, mentioned Sodom and Gomorrah and the wickedness that brought about their destruction. But neither rehearsed the nature of that wickedness. Paul, on the other hand, was the New Testament spokesman to the Greco-Roman world of his day. And it was a world in which homosexual practice was far more acceptable than among the Jews. Therefore it was natural that he would address the subject.

In Romans 1:18, he begins by speaking of how mankind had subverted and suppressed the truth by wickedness. It is a tale of cause and effect that should be profoundly instructive as we think about the natural human tendency to develop elaborate justifications for sin until it no longer appears like sin at all. There is danger in doing so from a position of needing to justify what one is already doing versus exploring what one might do.

Paul points out how these people had rejected the truth evident in nature and their own moral sense.

Therefore God gave them over in the sinful desires of their hearts to sexual impurity for the degrading of their bodies with one another. They exchanged the truth of God for a lie, and worshiped and served created things rather than the Creator—who is forever praised. Amen.

Because of this, God gave them over to shameful lusts. Even their women exchanged natural relations for unnatural ones. In the same way the men also abandoned natural relations with women and were inflamed with lust for one another. Men committed indecent acts with other men, and received in themselves the due penalty for their perversion (Rom. 1:24-27).

From that point on, it was downhill into every kind of wickedness, until they "not only continue to do these very things but also approve of those who practice them" (vs. 32).

This straightforward condemnation of homosexual behavior would stand unchallenged except for a modern twist. Gay theologians point out that the offenders Paul referred to as having "abandoned natural relations" *were* initially heterosexuals, and that is why they were called "perverts" when they changed. These gay advocates say they are not trying to change or pervert heterosexuals; all they want is the freedom for "inverts" or inborn homosexuals to do what's *natural* to them. In fact, they go one step further to say that efforts to change a person with a true homosexual inclination into a heterosexual is to *pervert* him or her and therefore wrong.

This interpretation cuts an imperceptibly fine line, which is in no way evident in the text, between the specific and the general. In this whole passage, Paul is not discussing some few individual men and women; he is speaking inclusively about how the whole godless and wicked population exchanged its knowledge of God for idols. The text says that natural relations were exchanged for unnatural ones involving "indecent acts" with same-sex partners. This in itself is what was unnatural, unnatural to the very fabric of creation.

An invert may feel that for him or her, homosexual behavior is natural. But that doesn't change things. Homosexuality is unnatural. And our assignment must be to discover how God's power can be employed to reverse the bad exchange that the homosexual has made.

One further observation about the Romans passage. In Chapter 1 Paul outlines the moral bankruptcy of the pagan world. Chapter 2 begins with these words of warning: "You, therefore, have no excuse, you who pass judgment on someone else, for at whatever point you judge the other, you are condemning yourself, because you who pass judgment do the same things" (vs. 1). Later in the chapter he points out that the Jews were just as bankrupt, even though they had the Law, because they were

25

hypocrites. Romans 3:10-12 says, "There is no one righteous, not even one; there is no one who understands, no one who seeks God. All have turned away, they have together become worthless; there is no one who does good, not even one." From there Paul introduces the solution: justification by faith.

The point made here and elsewhere in Scripture is that homosexual behavior does not have a more serious *spiritual* consequence than other sins. Sin, big or small, equally separates us from God. That's the spiritual truth. (Thankfully, another spiritual truth is that any sin, big or small, can be forgiven.)

But is there another reality which makes some sins more *dangerous* than others? Possibly. Romans 1:27 concludes by saying that the consequence of homosexual behavior was that the participants "received in themselves the due penalty for their perversion." There is no corresponding pronouncement about the Jews even though their faithlessness separated them equally from God. In addition to separating us from God (as do sins of the heart) violations of God's natural laws *also* result in natural, disastrous consequences. In a real sense, venereal disease and the AIDS epidemic are natural consequences of reckless sexual behavior. But so are unwanted pregnancies from extramarital sex. And as with all sin, innocent people—like hemophiliacs and babies—may also suffer the consequences of others' actions.

But more universal than these physical consequences (and therefore possibly more the point of Rom. 1:27) are the emotional and spiritual consequences. If some sins are more dangerous than others, it may be because some are more tenacious than others. Some interact so deeply with a person's psyche, that they are extremely hard to conquer. For instance, many find their first experience of sexual intercourse to be a deeply bonding event; that's the way God intended it. But if it occurs with someone other than the one a person marries, there may follow a long period of adjustment before the past can be forgotten. Or take those who get involved in drugs or the occult; they *do* enter into another world of sorts which often fights with reality for preeminence.

Is it any wonder that those who have embraced homosexual behavior find it extremely difficult to change? They've mixed the very emotional experience of sex with "another world" experience that ultimately involves their whole identity and life-style. And that's hard to forget, hard to leave behind. Could this partially result in the "due penalty for their perversion" that makes homosexual behavior so dangerous? We need to be careful that we never think of the person involved in homosexuality as more sinful than ourselves; that's the warning of Romans 2. But we must also not become desensitized to the danger of its abnormality.

4. Homosexual Behavior—Listed As Sin

Do you not know that the wicked will not inherit the kingdom of God? Do not be deceived: Neither the sexually immoral nor idolaters nor adulterers nor male prostitutes [malakoi] nor homosexual offenders [arsenokoitai] nor thieves nor the greedy nor drunkards nor slanderers nor swindlers will inherit the kingdom of God. And that is what some of you were. But you were washed, you were sanctified, you were justified in the name of the Lord Jesus Christ and by the Spirit of our God (*I Cor. 6:9-11*).

We also know that law is made not for the righteous but for lawbreakers and rebels, the ungodly and sinful, the unholy and irreligious; for those who kill their fathers or mothers, for murderers, for adulterers and perverts [arsenokoitais], for slave traders and liars and perjurers—and for whatever else is contrary to the sound doctrine that conforms to the glorious gospel of the blessed God, which he entrusted to me (*I Tim. 1:9-11*).

These two lists provide some specific insights. In I Corinthians Paul mentions both *malakoi* and *arsenokoitai* and the New International Version translates them quite precisely. *Malakoi* literally means "soft to the touch" and is frequently used in Greek literature to mean the effeminate or soft appearance cultivated by some men as part of their passive role in homosexual activities. *Arsenokoitai* comes from two words, *arsen* (male) and *koita* (coitus), so it is quite accurate to translate it as the homosexual offender, or the one taking the active role. In the I Timothy passage, the New International Version translates this last word simply as "pervert." It could have been translated more precisely. The Revised Standard Version translates it as "sodomites," for instance.

But maybe the most significant and hope-giving verse in either of these passages is I Corinthians 6:11: "And that is what some of you were. But you were washed, you were sanctified, you were justified in the name of the Lord Jesus Christ and by the

Spirit of our God.'' In spite of all the discouragement that a gay person may encounter in trying to change, and in spite of the insistence of some pro-gay groups that homosexuals can't change, here is proof that they can change. Some of these people had been involved in homosexual activity, but now they were not.

COMMUNICATING THE HOPE

People need hope before they'll ask for help. But they cannot have hope concerning a problem that no one is willing to discuss.

Mentioning the 'Unmentionable'

Pat Boone, the well-known singer who is also an evangelical Christian, may seem like an unlikely person to counsel a woman struggling with homosexuality, but this is, in fact, what happened. A young woman by the name of Joy desired to be free of her homosexual struggles, but she didn't know where to turn. One day she attended one of his concerts and was impressed by his Christian life-style. She concluded that his exposure to Hollywood's decadence also likely brought him into contact with homosexuals. So she wrote to Pat for advice on overcoming her own struggles. The story of that unique counseling relationship was detailed in the book, *Joy,* later titled, *Coming Out.*

One of our OUTPOST clients waited nearly two years to discuss his struggle with his pastor. He was waiting to hear the pastor's views on the subject before he risked any personal disclosure.

In my own church, the pastor *never* mentioned the word. Many times he would say things like, ''God has delivered some of you from drug addiction, alcoholism, prostitution, fornication, and every other kind of vile thing.'' Somehow, I hoped my sin was one of those other ''vile things,'' but I desperately wanted to hear him *say it.* And because I didn't, I began to read the Bible like he preached it. I viewed homosexuality as the ''unmentionable sin'' and figured that it was *so* abominable that God wouldn't even talk about it. I began reading with a filter. Scriptures like II Corinthians 5:17 (''Therefore, if anyone is in Christ, he is a new creation . . .'') had previously ministered hope, but now they were uncertainties. What if Paul meant everybody *except* the homosexual? As strange as it may sound, I really did begin thinking like that.

Homosexuality, I learned later, was not an unmentionable sin. Paul mentioned it in the verses we have looked at earlier. I Corinthians 6:9-11 became one of my favorite passages. Homosexuality was not at the top of the list as though it was the biggest, nor was it at the end as though it was nearly unmentionable. It was right in the middle. Plus, it said that there were *former* homosexuals. There was hope!

I'm not suggesting that pastors need to mention homosexuality in every sermon, but I am recommending that they mention it more often. I also believe that virtually every reference to homosexuality ought to be coupled with a reference to hope. Most homosexuals have no doubt that we call it sin (though some fight that designation), but what they need to hear is that we believe redemption is possible. One pastor displays a few well-chosen books on homosexuality on his library shelf. People who come to him for counsel know that he is at least familiar with the topic. (Note: A book on *Hope for Homosexuals* will encourage more people to open up than one called, *The Growing Gay Plague*.)

Patience! We're All Still Under Construction

However, as I grew in faith, I noticed some amazing things. For every Scripture that seemed to say that it was all over, there was another that talked about a daily fight. One Scripture said, "you died"; and another said, "put to death." One said that I was "new"; another said to "be renewed." One said that I had been "crucified with Christ," while another admonished me to "crucify the flesh." I soon began to realize the bittersweet coexistence of both *position* and *process*. Positionally, I was a new creature before God, but I was also still in the process of healing and maturity.

For some curious reason, this has been a major issue with homosexuality. With other sins, we seem to readily grasp this doctrinal dilemma, but with homosexuality, we want the renewal to be completed instantly. Some would even say, "If you're still tempted, then you're still a homosexual." Yet, this isn't the case with other sins. Biblically, I am no longer a homosexual or a homosexual offender, but I still have struggles with homosexual temptations.

For this reason, we avoid using the noun "homosexual" to refer to Christians who are breaking away from that sin. Often

29

we will use it as a descriptive adjective, such as "the homosexual individual." But even that is too limiting. Homosexuality is only one of many sins that they struggle with. Our descriptive phrase has since gotten lengthier as we describe "individuals who struggle with homosexuality." While it is more cumbersome than some shorter phrases, it is infinitely more accurate. I have questioned whether the apparent verbal gymnastics are really necessary, but then I have remembered that "identity conflicts" are often at the root of the problem anyway, as we'll see in Chapter 3. Perhaps identity is a good issue to be nit-picky about.

Frank Worthen, the founder of Love in Action, writes, "For the ex-gay person, change has definitely come. God has done a work in his life. Much is different: attitudes, desires, relationships with others. But the work is not complete. God still changes his life day by day. Even after God has completed the change in the area He's working on today, there will be areas left to be healed in some point in the future.

"Nowhere, though, does the Bible promise that a believer will come to the place where he or she is never tempted again. In fact, Scripture promises just the opposite: we will face a lifetime of trials and temptations. We are told to rejoice in our trials, for they build Christian maturity."[4]

What, Then, Does Change Mean?

The person who is struggling with a life-dominating sin, such as homosexuality, isn't just sinning because it brings pleasure. He or she is acting out of intense internal conflict. For such a person, sin does not represent pleasure as much as it represents survival. Allow me to illustrate this.

We are all familiar with the cigarette ads that represent smoking as a pleasurable relaxation . . . out in the country . . . after a good meal with good coffee and friends. People who smoke only for pleasure find it relatively simple to break the habit. Then there are others, those who grope for the cigarettes before they climb out of bed in the morning, who need three more before breakfast, and who bite their nails on the bus because they can't smoke there. There are reasons—more than the physical addiction to nicotine—why these people smoke. Is it any wonder that they have a more difficult time quitting?

Those "reasons" are the roots of the life-dominating behavior. For me it was a distorted sense of identity and poor self-worth that fed my homosexual desires. Even though I stopped acting on those desires, it was only as God helped me resolve the deeper internal conflicts that the dominion of the homosexual struggle in my life was broken. Even now, when I find myself tempted, it is always possible to trace it to the root causes.

I often define the hope that I offer homosexuals as "freedom from the *life-dominating effects* of homosexuality." That's the reality that I've found, and I think it is Biblical. The Bible doesn't promise freedom from temptation (though Jesus tells us to pray to not be tempted), but it does say, "For sin shall not have dominion over you" (Rom. 6:14, KJV).

CHAPTER THREE

DISCOVERING THE ROOTS OF HOMOSEXUALITY

WHILE PSYCHOLOGY WAS STILL VIEWING HOMOSEXUALITY as an "illness," a number of theories were in existence. Perhaps the most widespread of these was the "dominant mother" theory. It was commonly believed that the male homosexual had a close and binding attachment to a smothering mother. In this unnatural but nonsexual attachment, it was believed that the male never fully developed in his own masculine identity and, at times, could not relate to any woman other than his mother.

Another common theory held that homosexuality was, in fact, a hatred or contempt for women that precluded any sexual attachments to the opposite sex and resulted in an attachment for the same sex. Some have viewed homosexuality as a paranoid condition, while others recognize it as a problem of arrested development. The latter theory is largely based on Freud's theories of development and surmises that homosexual individuals have never grown beyond the Oedipal complex.

In recent years, the most commonly held view has been that of "constitutional" or "inborn" homosexuality. Many believe that there is a genetic or hormonal cause for the homosexual condition, although this has not been proven.

While many still hold to this theory, others refute it. The genetic theory of homosexuality has been generally discarded today. There is no proof to suggest a cause and effect relationship between homosexuality and hormone imbalance.

There is no reliable evidence that an endocrine difference exists between normal and homosexual. Castration doesn't cause homosexuality. Even injection of female hormones fails to make a man who has been normal behave in a homosexual way.

In commonly held theories, some are more acceptable to Christians then others. From my Christian perspective this is the best position, as I see it.

More recently, the theory of homosexuality as a "learned"

condition has been advanced. This theory suggests that sexual behavior is the cumulative result of the learning and conditioning he has had. He doesn't, according to this theory, start out with tendencies in one direction or the other.

Dealing with Self-Pity

As a psychologist with 20 years of practical counseling experience with homosexuals, Gerard Van Den Aardverg noted a prevailing sense of self-pity that plagued most of his clients. While many had experienced various types of rejection, it was the unwillingness to let go of the self-pity that fed their homosexual struggles.

In response to this, Van Den Aardverg introduced what he called "laugh therapy." He coached his clients into minimizing their self-pity by exaggerating it until it became ludicrous and something at which they could laugh. As they relinquished the self-pity, they soon began to rise above their problems and assume more personal responsibility for their own lives and their own decisions.

Identity Conflicts

Identity conflicts and the hurts of the past were the focus of Leanne Payne's book, *The Broken Image*, published by Crossway Books in 1981. As a practitioner of inner healing, she noted common roots among the homosexuals that she dealt with. Past hurts and conflicts, often not consciously retained, were producing sexual conflicts in these individuals. Through healing prayer and visualization sessions she sought to heal these past hurts and thereby resolve the identity conflicts.

Defensive Detachment

Dr. Elizabeth R. Moberly, a research psychologist from Cambridge, England, produced two separate books addressing essentially the same topic. *Psychogenesis: The Early Development of Gender Identity* (London: Routledge and Kegan Paul, Ltd., 1983) was addressed largely to the psychological community. *Homosexuality: A New Christian Ethic* (Cambridge: James Clarke and Co., Ltd., 1983) was written to help understand homosexuality from a Christian perspective. Dr. Moberly's theories in some ways marked a radical change from common theory and treatment, both Christian and secular. In *Ethic* she claims that "From amidst a welter of details, one constant underlying principle suggests itself: that the homosexual—whether man or woman—has suffered from some deficit in the relationship with the parent *of the same sex*; and that there is a corresponding drive to make good this deficit—through the medium of same-sex, or 'homosexual,' relationships."[1] She then goes on to describe how "defensive detachment" occurs in young children and the way it produces homosexual inclinations:

Needs for love from, dependency on, and identification with, the parent of the same sex are met through the child's attachment to the parent. If, however, the attachment is disrupted, the needs that are normally met through the medium of such an attachment remain unmet. Not merely is there a disruption of attachment, but, further, a defensive detachment. This resistance to the restoration of attachment (in analytic terms, counter-cathexis and not mere withdrawal of cathexis) is what marks the abiding defect in the person's actual relational capacity, that long outlasts the initial occasion of trauma. However, the repression of the normal need for attachment has to contend, like every repression, with the corresponding drive toward the undoing of repression—in this case, the drive toward the restoration of attachment. It is here suggested that it is precisely this reparative urge that is involved in the homosexual impulse, that is, that this impulse is essentially motivated by the need to make good earlier deficits in the parent-child relationship.[2]

What she is suggesting is that if a child experiences a hurtful break in the relationship with the same-sex parent, the child may withdraw defensively and resist future efforts at reconciliation; the child doesn't want to be hurt again. However, the child carries within a need for love from that same-sex parent creating a "reparative urge" that can be expressed as the homosexual drive.

Moberly makes it clear that this deficit is not necessarily the result of willful maltreatment (though it could be) and likewise she says, "The human situation is such that hurt may sometimes occur without it being a matter for blaming anyone."[3] She also points out that many times children genuinely get over hurtful situations. Not every child will respond the same way to the same situation.

One might also think that if Moberly's theory is true, there would be an exceptionally high incidence of homosexuality among children from single-parent families. "On the contrary," she says, "one notable study of male homosexuals indicates that only a small group had no father (Bieber *et al.*, 1962). Moreover, sometimes it will be the parent of the opposite sex who is missing; or the death or departure of the same-sex parent may come only relatively late in the child's process of growth; or the absence of a same-sex parent may not result in this particular kind of psychological deficit; or acceptable parent-substitutes may be found."[4]

All of these very complex dynamics simply indicate that humans don't respond in a deterministic fashion, but they let us begin to understand causes.

In addition to defensive detachment from the same-sex parent, Moberly also suggests that the child may experience impaired identity development. This may explain the instances of effeminacy in some male homosexuals and quasi-masculinity in some female homosexuals. Freud's mother fixation in male homosexuals, she suggests, may be a result of an abnormal detachment from the father rather than being itself a cause of the homosexuality.

While recognizing these origins of the homosexual urge, she does not condone the sexual expression of that urge. The true need is for identification and relationship, not sex, but this has gotten confused in the individual at the onset of puberty. "The psychological needs of the homosexual are often expressed sexually, but these needs exist independently of sexual expression. A good nonsexual relationship with a member of the same sex is another means of fulfilling such needs."[5] "An attachment to the same sex is not wrong, indeed it is precisely the right thing for meeting same-sex deficits. What is improper is the eroticization of the friendship."[6] Moberly points out that homosexual relationships fail to meet the basic need of each partner because both participants bring the same unmet needs to the relationship.

Therefore, based on Moberly's insights, here are some understandings and guidelines for treatment. No single book will qualify a person to treat homosexuality. As with any complex problem, a Christian helper needs experience, much time in prayer, and a variety of insights from other Christians. The annotated bibliography in this book will help.

1. "Homosexuality essentially involves a defect in the capacity for relating to the same sex—not the opposite sex, as is commonly assumed."[7] Therefore . . .

2. Attempted heterosexual relationships will not address the

basic problem.

3. The underlying problem is the defensive detachment and the unmet love needs and resulting identity impairment with the same-sex parent. Homosexual activities are only symptoms— futile attempts to meet those needs.

4. The first goal must be the undoing of the defensive detachment. This can be facilitated by insight, repentance and forgiveness, and healing of memories. But that is not enough . . .

5. God usually does not "cure" people of legitimate needs. Therefore, the second goal is the making up of those unmet needs, and that can happen only through relationships.

6. Nonsexual, same-sex relationships with someone mature enough to keep it nonsexual can be helpful.

7. Though sexual expressions should be resisted, occasions of homosexual urges are opportunities to discover and deal with the legitimate, underlying needs.

We must continue to remember that this is a pioneer field. There is some disagreement, for example, over whether a person is born to *attain* heterosexuality (as Moberly holds) or is heterosexual at birth. These are comparatively insignificant differences in some developing theories, however, and our focus ought to be on areas of agreement. Whether a person is born heterosexual or born *to become* heterosexual, God's purpose remains the same.

Dealing with the Roots

I had not heard of Moberly back in 1979 and 1980 when I was doing my initial work on the "roots of homosexuality." And yet my own experience and thinking largely paralleled hers. At that time I had not considered that I was actually laying out theory. Quite simply, I was just attempting to explain the dynamics of the homosexual struggle in my own life and as I witnessed it in the lives of the several hundred counselees with whom I had worked.

My basic premise was rooted in the Bible. Though the Bible clearly identifies homosexuality as sinful, it is given no special treatment to distinguish it spiritually from other sins. In the New Testament passages such as I Corinthians 6:9 and 10, and I Timothy 1:9 and 10, the sin is listed in the midst of other, more "common" sins. Furthermore, I Corinthians states, "And that is what some of you were," clearly indicating that it was a sin that people had overcome in Bible days. Recognizing it as a life-dominating problem, I began paying special attention to both Christian and secular treatment for other compulsive behaviors. I noted that most compulsive behaviors could be traced to a variety of root problems, usually of an emotional nature, that fed the more visible compulsion.

Initially, I discovered nine root problems that commonly occurred either in my life or the lives of my clients. These roots were *rejection, rebellion, fear, self-pity, envy, bitterness, deception, moral impurity,* and *oppression.* I further noted that these roots acted both as initial catalysts (helping to create the homosexual problem itself) and as current aggravators (promoting fresh struggles).

The more I considered these roots, the more the issue of *rejection* seemed to be the taproot. An individual often developed a homosexual identity in response to being rejected by family, siblings, peers, or society. Even after that reaction was understood and dealt with, a habit response remained that could create new struggles. A fresh experience of rejection (which everyone faces from time to time) would habitually result in strong homosexual temptations. As the principal root, rejection created a problem of broken identity and fed several of the other roots, as well.

For instance, *rebellion* is an inability to trust—possibly because significant others have proved untrustworthy. And if "perfect love drives out fear," as I John 4:18 says, then, I surmised, does the absence of love (which obviously accompanies rejection) create fear?

Self-pity, with its message of "nobody loves me; everybody hates me" is plain to see as closely related to rejection. *Envy* is based in low self-esteem or self-rejection and the desire to be more acceptable. *Bitterness* is usually a response to a hurt or rejection experience. *Moral impurity* (a fascination with sexual things) reduces sex to an experience rather than a relationship; it often grips those who feel a relationship is impossible. *Spiritual oppression* is the only one of the original roots that doesn't have (at least for some people) a direct connection to rejection. Occasionally, even it can be traced to rejection.

When I came across Moberly's writings approximately five years later, I immediately noticed that rejection (either real or imagined) by the same-sex parent was identified by Moberly as the primary cause for homosexuality. The fact that I had seen its manifestation in the nine roots was completely compatible with Moberly's theory. Furthermore, her suggestion that, for the homosexual, there had been a *very early* experience of rejection, explained why many heterosexuals were able to endure rejections in later life without it stimulating homosexual urges in them.

Synthesizing these concepts has provided a very effective approach to understanding and ministering to those who struggle with homosexuality. Through effective counselors and mature Christian relationships in the church, the homosexual can receive the love which was unmet in early childhood because of the initial experience of rejection. Then, direct attention to the "roots" in later years and in the present can bring further freedom.

Other Factors

While some slight differences exist between the preceding theories, each considers homosexuality as a learned condition, and therefore one that can be *unlearned*. However, the Moberly model that places the exclusive cause on a break in the relationship between the child and the same-sex parent may be too narrow. Both Leanne Payne and I believe that other experiences of rejection or other kinds of trauma may also result in the homosexual condition. Such factors as sexual abuse, rape, molestation, pornography, and peer rejection can play significant roles in the development of a homosexual identity.

Sexual Abuse

The incidence of sexual abuse, particularly incest, among lesbians is alarmingly high. In our counseling experience, we have learned that many were victims of incest involving a male member of the family, whether that was the father, a brother, an uncle, or a cousin. These experiences are particularly devastating because these are the very men that a woman should have been able to trust. They are the men who should have protected her from the abuse of others. But when the "protectors" prove untrustworthy and become the assailants, all of reality gets turned upside down. The emotional damage can be very severe.

Other lesbians were traumatized by rape or by being "used" sexually by males. At times, this resulted in a traumatic sexual dysfunction. For others it resulted in the simple conclusion that men "are only after one thing." Many women become lesbians because they believe that it is the only way that they will find a gentle, loving, sexual experience.

Males who have been victims of sexual abuse can develop homosexually for other reasons. Most have been abused by other males and are confused over why it happened to them. They may wonder if they "sent out signals" to attract the incident, or they may wonder why they were not able to resist the abuse, and, at times, they may worry why their own bodies responded sexually to the assault. This confusion and worry seems, in some cases, to have been the source for the person beginning to conclude that he was homosexual.

Pornography

The effect of pornography, in my opinion, whether direct or indirect, should not be minimized. For women, pornography targeted at males may only reinforce the belief that all men "are only after sex." For males, pornography can produce a variety of responses.

I recall that my own early exposure to pornography created a number of dilemmas. It seemed to me that the *women* presented a challenge to my masculinity. When I thought of sex I imagined a relationship, not an encounter, but the women portrayed in the pornography were intimidating. They seemed to know everything about sex, while I was still unsure about it. At the same time, I could not relate to the men. For the most part, they were seductive, experienced, and well endowed, while I was none of these. I envied them, but I also despised them. At times, I wished that "I had what they had." Sometimes this desire became sexually confused until I thought I wanted *them,* not what they possessed. (It should be noted that these same ideas are also promoted to some degree by advertising, television, and locker-room talk.)

Peer Rejection

My work has shown me that peer relationships and peer pressure are also able to play their roles in the formation of a homosexual identity. We have strong and rigid standards for what it means to be male. The male who has no desire to play childhood games such as war, jailbreak, and cowboys and Indians is often called names and ostracized—even though these activities have little to do with real manhood. Cultural messages such as "boys don't cry," "men don't quit," and "guys are tough" feed this problem, also. Women face their own list of what it means in our society to be female.

In my first years of counseling, a fair percentage of our clients came from the University of Minnesota. Most of these were young men who had been raised in Christian homes in small towns. As they shared their stories with me, I discovered that they were never taught and prepared to cope with the fact that they might be counted different from the world. When they got to the university, they discovered that they were not like the other guys. They were not "party animals." Their morals prevented them from "sleeping around." While they had had no previous problems with homosexuality, they began to doubt their heterosexuality simply because they did not live for weekend beer busts and casual sex! This, in itself, portrays the incredible power of peer pressure.

Permissiveness

Another factor that needs to be considered is the growing sexual permissiveness that is occurring in our society. There is often a thrill from experiencing the "forbidden." This feeling can intensify the sexual gratification of a heterosexual engaging in homosexual behavior. And the source of that intensification may be erroneously attributed to the homosexual aspect of the encounter. That is to say, some individuals, who otherwise may be completely heterosexual, may question their sexual orientation based on this excitement of the forbidden.

CHAPTER FOUR

CASE STUDIES:
SITUATIONS YOU MAY FACE

THIS CHAPTER PROVIDES SEVERAL STORIES OF PEOPLE WHO have struggled with homosexuality. Some have changed, and some have not. But the purpose of telling the stories is to give you, as a pastor or ministering Christian, examples of the kinds of situations you may encounter. The stories also provide you the opportunity to consider some of the approaches for counseling.

The struggles are real, but to preserve confidentiality, each story is a composite of more than one person. All names and other identifying characteristics have been changed.

Uncurtailed Curiosity

Andy was a young man who had just moved to the city from a small town. Raised in a Christian home, he was somewhat mesmerized by the fast-paced, urban life. As he began to compare himself with other guys at the college he attended, he began sensing he was different. He didn't relate to the crudeness, carousing, and sexual carrying on of the typical fraternity type. At the same time, he began to learn about the "gay life" in that city.

He called a Christian ministry to gays because his curiosity was getting out of hand. He found himself venturing into places where gays were rumored to hang out and he wasn't sure what he would do if someone propositioned him.

He talked at length about these issues with a counselor, but his curiosity remained. Week after week, he reported some "new" thing that he had done—going into a gay bar, attending a gay movie, going to the gay beach. Although he started out as a curious observer, he soon got involved in homosexual activities. Each experience was unfulfilling, but he kept thinking that he hadn't experienced enough.

One day he called his counselor in distress. While he never identified himself as a homosexual, he had fallen in love with another man. He was filled with self-contempt and guilt.

The counselor was getting increasingly emotionally involved with the client's progress. The client seemed honest and sincere. For the most part, he really did want "out," but he kept playing around the edges and got ensnared. The counselor spent hours at a time with the young man, trying to help him see what was going on, but curiosity and, eventually, his own selfishness took over. He moved from one lover to the next and finally decided to pursue a gay life-style wholeheartedly.

The counselor was shaken for months, wondering whether he failed, what he should have said. Should he have given more, and, if so, what? Maybe he didn't belong in the ministry. Finally, with perspectives brought by the supervisor and fellow counselors, he came to see that he was not a "rescuer." All he could hope to do was help. All the counsel and wisdom one has can never override a person's will. For some people, all of the time and emotional investment that humanly could be offered will not produce change. The ultimate decision for change lies with the client. Even God will not override a person's will.

After seven years, Andy is still involved in the gay life-style.

Sex Without Love

Bernice was a beautiful girl, slender and popular. As a cheerleader in high school, she had dated boys from the football team and had consented to having sex with several of them. After high school, she started working downtown and became close friends with a girl at work. One night as she stayed over at her new friend's house, the friend began making sexual advances. Although she was initially frightened and repulsed, she was also excited and curious. Her friend led her through a night of "tender lovemaking."

Though she felt it was wrong, whenever Bernice felt lonely or hurt, she found herself spending more time with her new friend. Sometimes they would simply talk and "cuddle"; other times, sex entered the picture. Bernice started enjoying it more and more. While she still dated men, she always went back to her new friend whenever things started to sour.

When she finally went for counseling, she was extremely confused. In many ways her relationship with her friend had been far more loving and tender than the sexual encounters she had had in high school. Even though she was finally dating

Christian men, she felt that they, too, would "use her" like those other guys had; some of them had even tried. To Bernice, heterosexuality had come to mean "sex without love"; with lesbianism, she thought it was "sex with love."

On one level she sensed it was wrong, but on the other it was intensely satisfying. Even though she had broken off her relationship with her friend, it seemed that new relationships were always waiting for her. She entered Bible school, but even there she had found several other girls with whom she had sexual experiences.

Bernice's counselor was a man, but because he had been gay himself and could therefore talk more personally about the problem, she didn't feel threatened by him. As they talked and dealt with some of her generalizations about men, Bernice began to believe that there could be a loving, heterosexual relationship out there somewhere, but she still felt that it could never be as emotionally satisfying as a relationship with another woman.

In some ways, initially at least, this was true. As a woman, she had a natural, instant affinity with other women. They understood her monthly cycle. She didn't have to explain herself to them because they experienced the same things she had; they instantly understood.

"That," her counselor explained, "is one of the challenges of heterosexuality. It isn't two starting out as one, but rather, two *becoming one*. The heterosexual picture in the Bible is of two people growing closer and closer over the years, not instantly." Her counselor went on to explain that that may have been the reason she tired of her new lesbian lovers so easily. The relationship would start intensely intimate, and then in a few months the friction would start. "Perhaps you are too much alike," the counselor suggested.

The road has not been easy for Bernice. She still feels awkward in her relationships with most men, and she still has a tendency toward emotional dependency with other women. While she has stopped having sex with women, she is still "romantic" in other ways. She excessively sends cards and little gifts to her "special friend." She has one friend that she spends nearly every free moment with. Sometimes they hug and kiss, but neither one feels that this is wrong—as long as it doesn't lead to sex.

While her counselor has tried to explain how this is an over-dependent relationship, Bernice doesn't yet see it. "Both of us are praying more than we ever did," Bernice protests. But most of Bernice's prayers, it seems, are for her friend and their friendship. While some progress has been made, Bernice has a long way to go.

Identity Crisis

Many times the individuals who come for counsel are struggling with nothing more than an identity crisis, either temporary or long-lived. Bob was one of those. He had never had any homosexual experience but had become fascinated with "macho men." His struggles involved looking at men on the streets, sneaking looks at the "hunk" calendars that were available in many bookstores, and some occasional fantasy.

A homosexual man had made his acquaintance and Bob was fighting with feelings toward this man. This motivated him to ask for help.

Bob's case was a counselor's dream. He had a strong Christian commitment, and he knew that homosexuality was wrong. After only one session, it was clear to both him and the counselor that his problems were rooted in his own identity conflicts and a lack of assertiveness. Bob was physically a small man, quiet and well mannered. He had also lost his father at an early age.

He quickly realized that the "macho-man" image that attracted him represented both the physical build and the emotional temperament that he wished he had. While there was nothing he could do about his physical stature, his counselor began reinforcing his image of himself as a man. Weren't his Christian convictions, even in the face of his struggles, a mark of silent strength? Was it unmanly to be quiet and well mannered? His counselor identified for him Biblical models of men, such as Moses, who possessed these qualities.

After just a few counseling sessions, Bob no longer needed regular counseling services. Over the years he keeps in touch with the ministry, sometimes needing a "boost," but he has never fallen into homosexual behavior and is living a fulfilled Christian life.

A Way to Escape

In many ways Carl was at the other extreme from Bob. Although he was a Christian and believed that homosexual behavior was wrong, he got involved sexually nearly once a week. Week after week the story was the same: "I was just sitting in my apartment and decided to go for a walk; the next thing I knew I was in the pornographic bookstore." Sometimes the ultimate destination changed, but the pattern was always the same.

The counseling goals with Carl were twofold: one was to discover his hidden motivations; the other was to build hope. Carl's personal dynamics were explored with questions like: What were you thinking while you were still in your apartment? What happened at work that day? Where did you tell yourself that you were going? When did you realize that you were heading for trouble?

His answers gave the clues for subsequent therapy. Sometimes he was feeling lonely, sometimes depressed. Sometimes he was not even aware of what he was feeling, but his workday offered some clues. The boss had yelled at him; he messed up on a task; someone made fun of him; someone called him "gay." Each of these led to feelings of rejection or inadequacy.

The counselor posed additional questions designed to help him build "roadblocks." This was done with the conviction that every temptation *does* have its "way of escape." However, quite often a person is moving too fast to notice it. Therefore, it can help to place roadblocks, barriers, and warning signs along your usual temptation route.

Sometimes Carl was so caught up in his emotional problems that he just "walked and walked"; his feet often took the same old route and carried him to his old sin hangouts. Many times, when Carl realized where he was heading, he would get even more despondent, thinking, "Look at me, on top of everything else, I'm heading for the bookstore." Rather than fight the feeling or alter his course, he would get lost in this new bad feeling, too.

Due to the complexity of Carl's problems, it didn't take months, it took *years* to unravel his problems. Patiently (and sometimes not), his counselor attacked his emotional problems and reflexes one at a time. Slowly Carl developed his awareness of the warning signs: going for a walk with no destination, heading toward downtown instead of another direction, the street sign of the street where the bookstore was, etc.

Carl was reminded again and again of the reality that there is *always* "a way of escape." Although it was easier to resist some temptations while he was still inside his apartment, there was always a way of escape along the way. He could turn around when he got to the corner, or perhaps when he finally realized where he was heading. Even if he arrived at the bookstore or bar, he didn't have to go inside. If he went inside, he could leave without indulging. Even if he went so far as to buy something or meet someone, he could throw the stuff away or tell the person he'd changed his mind. It was important that he not be trapped into thinking, "Well, I've gone this far so I might as well give in."

Building hope was also essential. Carl's ongoing struggles were more frustrating to him than they were to his counselor. So his counselor constantly reinforced him by showing him the areas where he was making progress. The counselor talked about not only the times he failed but the times that he wanted to sin but didn't.

Today, Carl is happily married and has been so for four years. He and his wife have a little toddler. Carl calls his counselor each spring. In the spring, he tends to experience a fresh wave of temptation when everyone starts running around with some of their clothes off. But other than that, he claims to have very little struggle with homosexuality, and is very much in love with his wife. He finds his sexual relationship with her to be very satisfying.

An Over-dependent Relationship

Cassie is a pastor's wife. A young woman in the church came to her about a year ago for general counseling, and they became close friends. After several months, the young woman confided that she had a homosexual background. Cassie, in godly love for her, tried to help. But once, after a lengthy prayer time, as Cassie hugged her friend, she felt some erotic stirrings herself. This frightened her and she went to a ex-gay ministry counseling center.

Her first concern, of course, was whether she was somehow a latent homosexual. It was reassuring to her to learn that an erotic response to an inappropriate situation did not mean she had a basic problem with homosexuality. Such a response could have occurred to anyone under those circumstances. What needed attention was bringing some order to the relationship.

Cassie wasn't sure what to do. The friendship, by her own admission, had gotten out of hand. Her friend called or stopped by every day, often spending hours at a time with her. At church functions, the friend was always at her side. Cassie felt her other friendships being stifled. She didn't want to reject her friend, but she wanted some freedom, too. The friend refused to go to the center for counseling but usually called Cassie immediately after Cassie's appointments to find out what had been talked about.

The counselor advised Cassie that she needed to be more firm with her friend. How did she handle her three year old when she demanded too much attention or wanted attention at the wrong times? Cassie smiled when she realized that her friend was, in fact, behaving much like her three year old. The counselor suggested that Cassie write down her priorities and decide how much time she could "freely" give her friend. She had to realize that her friend might get upset with her at times, but that didn't mean she wasn't giving her the most appropriate and helpful attention she could.

After several months, Cassie confided that "setting limits" actually saved the friendship. "I was feeling so choked," she admitted, "that I'm sure I would have ended the whole friendship by now."

Instant Deliverance

Dan went to a counseling center not because he thought he needed any counseling but to tell the staff of his amazing deliverance and to volunteer his services to pray with and counsel others.

He had met the Lord three months previously and had been prayed for. In his words, he was "an entirely new creature." He even had plans to be married soon. He was full of stories of God's amazing power and the miracles he had seen.

When the staff questioned him about whether he still had temptations, Dan quoted II Corinthians 5:17, "Therefore, if anyone is in Christ, he is a new creation; the old has gone, the new has come!" When asked if his fiancée knew of his homosexual past, Dan said he had told her that he had struggled with it in his "past." Dan felt ready to enter a ministry so that he could share the "good news" with others who had that same problem. He was brimming with enthusiasm and hope.

It was not easy "bursting his bubble," and, in fact, some

wondered if it was proper to do so. Perhaps he *had* been instantly delivered. God is certainly capable of doing that. But the staff had its questions. Usually Satan moves in through an already opened door and plays on weaknesses people already have. Those weaknesses usually need time to heal and strengthen.

What problems did Dan have that *preceded* his crisis? What personal weaknesses had Satan played on? Had he been marred by personal rejection? Did he have an unhealthy relationship with his parents? If so, what steps had he taken to deal with these issues?

Dan grew angry with the center's staff as they began to probe these sensitive areas, and soon he walked out. But the story has a happier ending. He returned a year later, a little less sure of his "theology" and a good deal more dependent on the Lord. His problem areas were leading to homosexual struggles and to problems in his marriage. It seemed every time his wife was not completely pleased with something that Dan did, he would clam up for days. During that time, he admitted, he struggled with homosexual fantasies, and on two occasions had played out those fantasies.

What had happened to his "deliverance"? He was shaken and ready for some help.

It turned out that his main root problem was bitterness. He was actually bitter at many people in his past, but the most predominant resentment was toward a very demanding mother, whom he felt he could never please. He grew to hate her, and that hatred found its revenge for him in exchanging a natural interest in women for one in men.

Not knowing the habit she triggered, his wife sometimes expressed disappointment in his imperfections. Her complaints and ways of expressing them were fairly normal. But they somehow reminded Dan of his mom, and off he would go, down the path of bitterness he had never acknowledged or dealt with.

True deliverance began to be experienced as this pattern was discovered. Dan first had to confess and deal with his resentment toward his mother and a few other significant persons in his life. Then he and his wife were shown how to catch the sequence before it erupted into homosexual temptations. As it turned out, the first symptom was when Dan would go silent. Working together, they made progress toward true deliverance.

Incest

When Donna first went for counseling, she had trouble making eye contact. Often she would not speak above a whisper. Even as a Christian, she had been involved regularly in lesbian relationships. For several weeks her counselor discussed both her family relationships and her lesbian involvements. Her family seemed quite normal; they were all churchgoers and her dad served as a deacon. Beyond that, though, Donna had little to say.

However, her counselor began to notice that whenever her family was mentioned, Donna's countenance would change. Usually she hung her head a bit or cast a furtive glance toward the door. Finally her counselor asked if she had ever been involved sexually with any of her family members. Suddenly, Donna burst into tears.

One day, when she was 13, her dad had sexually molested her by fondling her breasts. The following year, one of her brothers had talked her into having sex with him. While this had all happened over ten years ago, she was still tortured by the guilt and shame.

"I still go to church but it's all a game," she said. "Whenever I see my dad in church acting like a good Christian, I get physically sick. I don't pray much, either," she admitted. "I can't understand why God let this happen to me."

As Donna and her counselor talked about forgiveness, Donna suddenly raised her voice. "Never! Never! I hope they both rot in hell." It took several weeks before she would even consider the option of forgiveness.

One day her counselor suggested a minor revelation to her. "Your dad and your brother both hurt you very badly, didn't they? Well, you know something? They're still doing it. It's been ten years, and you are still letting them ruin your life. Doesn't that make you mad enough to forgive them—so *you* can get on with *your* life?" It wasn't the best way to start the process of forgiveness, but it was a start.

As Donna continued in her counseling, she was also referred to a local ministry that dealt with victims of sexual abuse. In the group she met others who had also been sexual victims, and her grief, pain, and shame all flooded out in the second meeting.

Although she still bears the emotional scars of the abuse, she is getting on with her life. And giving up her resentment toward her father, brother, and even God, produced a major breakthrough of a growing freedom from homosexual temptation. She found a new church and began to experience some real joy in her Christian walk. While she is not yet ready to date men, she has found that she is able to talk to men more comfortably.

Unfinished Adolescence

Edward was a married man with two teen-age children. Although he had had some adolescent homosexual experiences and some strong homosexual longings, he had never gotten involved in adult homosexuality. In the year before he went for help, however, he had found the homosexual urges rising again and began buying gay magazines. Neither his wife nor children knew about his struggles and, in many ways, he felt trapped. He loved his wife but he was finding sex with her to be less satisfying. After all this time, he began to think that he had made a serious mistake in marrying her.

It was difficult to determine which problem fed which. Did the marriage pressures lead to a reemergence of his homosexual struggles, or did the homosexual struggles create the problems in his marriage? In some ways that question wasn't all that important. The fact was that Edward did have a wife and two children.

Edward and his wife had communication problems outside of the sexual ones. Most of their marriage difficulties were the "standard" type. The counselor at the ex-gay ministry encouraged him to seek joint counseling for both him and his wife, and told him that the homosexual issue probably would not need to come up there. (It gets too easy to blame that for everything.) While they pursued marriage counseling together, the ministry dealt with Edward on his sexual struggles.

The counselor learned that Edward had never really dealt with his earlier identity conflicts but, like many, had buried them. Now that his children were coming home with their own adolescent problems and pressures, Edward was being reminded of his own conflicts from his adolescence. He wondered if he would somehow pass on his homosexual struggles to his son. How could he help his son through any adolescent conflicts when he hadn't really dealt with his own?

As he began to review his own identity conflicts, Edward discovered that envy and fear loomed large. He had felt he was unlike other men and older boys as he grew up in both his abilities and appearance. A lot of his homosexual longings were motivated by a desire to be like other men. But he didn't realize this, and so over the years it became a recurring thing.

Edward's son appeared to be more "with it" than Edward had been, and yet every young person goes through stages of seeming more or less awkward and socially out of place. Edward worried that he had never provided his son a model or a method of facing such struggles, and that triggered the old feelings of failure and ineptitude.

In spite of the fact that Edward could articulate some of these fears regarding his own son—that he had been a poor masculine model for him—he had not been able to make the connection to his own unresolved identity conflicts surrounding envy and fear. Once Edward was able to see what had for so long been repressed in his own mind, he was able to apply the various spiritual principles to these roots, and that began to relieve him slowly of the homosexual pressures.

Rejection

Fred was a pastor with a vital church. He had had some homosexual struggles in his adolescence, but had not had any behavioral experiences since his early 20's. Then he met a young man in his church who also had a homosexual weakness. Relieved to find someone that he could share his struggles with, Fred and the young man became close friends and fell sexually once. Although Fred repented in great anguish, the young man went to another pastor for help in working through the trauma. The other pastor confronted Fred, and Fred resigned his pastorate. In the process, Fred confided the real problem to his wife, Ann, and she promised to stand by him.

Fred was overwhelmed by guilt and shame over the fact that he fell with someone in his own congregation, and felt that his ministry was over. He wanted to serve God, but he wasn't sure about anything anymore.

When Fred went in for counseling, his counselor began by reminding Fred of the things that he could be "sure of." His wife, for one thing, loved him deeply enough to stand by him. Although she knew his struggles, she still believed in him. That awareness comforted him, and he began to confide even more in his wife. The counselor asked Fred if he might also speak with her, both privately and together with him, to help her through this difficult time. Usually a sensitive man, Fred had overlooked the emotional stress that she was undergoing.

Ann was relieved to have someone to talk to. Although she was coping fairly well, she had begun to get bitter over the fact that Fred had someplace to go and she didn't. This problem had affected her deeply, too. She loved Fred and wanted to help, but she didn't know how. She had been looking for people she could talk to, but in her desire to protect Fred, she couldn't find anyone she could really trust.

In some ways, Ann confided, she was also relieved to finally know what the problem was. She had always known that there was something Fred wouldn't or couldn't share with her. She could sense his pain and frustration; she could see him beginning to withdraw, but she didn't know what it was or why. Now that she knew, she was encouraged. "Together," she said, "I think we can face anything; it's only when he withdraws that I feel so powerless."

The root of Fred's homosexual struggles was found in his symptom of withdrawal, which is often a first-line coping mechanism for rejection. Fred had never sensed the security of his relationship with his dad. Also, because he took his Christian commitment so seriously as a young boy, he often felt ostracized from his peers. He was called names and seen as too much of a goody-goody. He began a pattern of withdrawal at a very young age. He had no one to talk to about this and to help him interpret that rejection as suffering for Christ's sake, and therefore he internalized it as rejection of himself.

It took some time to convince Fred that he wasn't finished with God. Fred still has struggles with pain and frustration; he still has a tendency to withdraw. Ann relates that she still senses his pain, frustration, and withdrawal, but now she knows how to pray for him and respond to him.

The 'Enabler' Wife

When Gail went to a counseling center, she was nearly hysterical. Her husband had just told her that he was gay, and that he had determined he wanted that to be his open life-style. She confided that she had known something was wrong for a long time, but she felt like a fool because she had never suspected homosexuality. She even knew the other man and had had him over for dinner several times. To her, they were just bowling buddies.

She felt hopeless, alone, and very hurt that her husband had deceived her for so long. "All this time, I thought I knew him," she sobbed. It became clear very quickly that her husband had no desire to change, but Gail still clung to some threads of hope. Once, after he had announced his intentions, he had told her that he loved her. Another time he reminded her that she was still a very good friend.

The counselor helped Gail work through her hurt and the feeling that she was a fool. She encouraged Gail to begin to develop a life outside of her marriage, through friends and church. She even encouraged her to consider a trial separation.

"Oh, I could never leave him. He really depends on me, and that's my only hope. It's my way of loving him. How else could I ever hope to win him back?"

Gail thought that if she would just endure this thing, eventually she would "wake up" and her husband would be there like she had always wanted.

The counselor recommended a few books to her that were written for spouses of alcoholics and asked her to report on what she thought of them in their next session.

"You're trying to tell me that I'm an 'enabler,' aren't you?" she said the next time she went in. As she thought more about it, she realized that by making it too easy for her husband, she was actually facilitating his behavior. She had been giving him all the benefits of a marriage plus an outside affair. Finally, she agreed to a trial separation.

It's been three years. Slowly, Gail has started forming a life of her own, apart from him. She hardly ever gets depressed anymore, and when she does, she calls the counseling center or gets together with another spouse who is going through the same thing, but she still believes that someday her husband will come home.

No True Repentance

Although he attended church regularly, Ivan led a double life. Smiling and singing on Sunday morning, he was frequently "cruising" a gay park by evening. Sometimes he had three sexual partners in one night, and yet by the time he went in for counseling, he felt assured of God's forgiveness and was sure that it would never happen again.

This pattern of outrageous behavior and then claiming God's

forgiveness and being confident that it was all over continued for over a year. Despite the counselor's efforts, it seemed he could never get beyond the surface with Ivan. Ivan "spiritualized" the entire situation and was convinced that all was well.

The counselor tried to get him involved with a different local clinic dealing with "sexual addiction." This was a clinic that dealt with very severe compulsive sexual behaviors, and the counselor felt that he needed to confront Ivan with the fact that he was really sick before Ivan would take his problems seriously. But Ivan didn't believe this was necessary. The news of his sexual escapades was slowly leaking out, and many were asking the staff at the ex-gay ministry what they were doing about it.

Finally they informed Ivan that it was not enough to come in for weekly sessions—he could not return until he followed their advice about getting involved with the other clinic.

Ivan has not yet returned.

Danger for Counselors

Joe went in for counseling with a variety of emotional problems and detailed his obsession with strong, masculine men. At first the counseling seemed to be making good progress, when Joe suddenly confided that he was falling in love with his counselor. Eyeing his counselor cautiously, he wondered aloud if that would have any effect on the counseling relationship. "Not much," the counselor replied to Joe's amazement. "Your being in love with me isn't really a sexual thing at all," the counselor said. "I think you're in love with me because I'm helping you and you know I care. For that, I'm flattered. I'm also glad that you told me because it shows that you trust me. That's a good sign."

What could have been disastrous was suddenly brought down to scale. In a few weeks, Joe worked through his feelings, and he admitted later that he was glad that the counselor (whom he knew had come out of a gay life-style) didn't respond sexually. That wasn't really what he wanted or needed.

Wounded Parents

Initially it was Emily who called the counseling center to confide that she had just learned that their 18-year-old son was a homosexual. Throughout the phone conversation, she asked about the program and how it could help her son. As she was about to hang up, the counselor asked how *she* was holding up, and how this was affecting her. "I guess I need some help, too," she said quietly. An appointment was made for the following day. She was willing to talk.

A well-dressed woman, Emily fidgeted nervously in the waiting room. Before the counselor had closed the door to his office, Emily inquired, "Is it *always* the mother's fault? I feel so terrible."

"Not entirely," the counselor replied. "There seems to be a variety of causes."

The counselor related his own story in which he had had very little negative influence from his family. Then he told Emily of a conversation he had with his mother before entering the ministry. "My mother made what was intended as a positive statement, but her false guilt leaked through like a river. 'Honey,' she had said, 'I'm glad that even though your father and I made such a mess of things, God was able to straighten it out.' " The counselor had responded to his mother that blame, if there was any, was a two-way street. Sure, his parents weren't perfect, but they had meant well. He told how he hadn't been perfect, either, how he hadn't communicated his fears and problems very well. This seemed to set Emily at ease, and she was able to talk about some real issues of guilt that she felt. The counselor then reminded her that the Bible had a remedy for guilt, and that she didn't need to hold onto it forever.

After a while she began talking about her husband, Kevin. While she constantly affirmed what a good provider he was, she admitted that there had never been a strong relationship between him and this son.

"How does he feel about all of this?" the counselor asked.

"He doesn't want to talk about it," she replied. "We even had a fight about my coming here. He says it's a private matter."

That night, as they prepared for bed, Kevin asked Emily how it went, and Emily rambled on excitedly about the meeting. "Maybe," she said, "we could both go in sometime." It took several weeks for Kevin to decide to come in with his wife.

As nervous as Emily was that first time, Kevin was twice as nervous. As the counselor tried to talk about issues of guilt and shame that Kevin might be feeling, Emily kept interjecting all of his good points. Finally the counselor asked if he might talk with Kevin privately. Emily readily agreed.

"So you were one, too?" Kevin asked the counselor, when Emily was out of the room. "Didn't you even think of what it might do to your family? This thing is tearing Emily apart."

"But what about you? Surely this has got to be tough on you, too."

Kevin responded with a wave of anger and embarrassment. "I gave that kid everything. I even worked two jobs so he could go off to that foolish design school. I probably loved him too much."

Kevin's voice betrayed embarrassment when using the word "love"; it didn't roll off his tongue easily. "Did you ever tell him you loved him?" the counselor asked. "How often did you do things with him?"

Although he appeared to be on the verge of tears, Kevin kept his composure. "I never knew how to tell him," he confessed. "He was different, you know. He was always involved in things I knew nothing about—like this design stuff—but I bought him the best tools I could find. Now he goes and does this. I just don't understand."

As they talked, the counselor told Kevin that this wasn't just something his son was doing to get back at him or to punish him. "It sounds to me like he's still looking for the love he felt he didn't get from you," the counselor suggested. "Of course, it isn't quite that simple, but that might be part of it." He asked Kevin what the chances were of him and his son having a heart-to-heart talk. Kevin acknowledged that it would be possible but not too pleasant. The counselor warned him that although the talk would be long overdue, he shouldn't expect an instant response.

They had the talk a few weeks later.

Although their son is still involved in the gay life, the family communicates more openly. Kevin and Emily even discussed their concerns for him both spiritually and physically due to his homosexual involvements. Once he even promised to read some material they got for him. He said it was interesting, but he wasn't sure just yet. To Kevin and Emily, that's a sign of some real progress.

Unmotivated Son

Larry and Fran showed up at the office without an appointment. Larry was 16; Fran was his mother. As Larry sat sullenly in a chair, Fran said, "I hope somebody can talk some sense into him; I had to drag him in here as it is."

Before the counselor invited Larry into his office, he told both Larry and Fran that *all* the counseling was private, that he wouldn't be able to tell Fran anything that Larry said. Any disclosures between them would be purely up to Larry. Although Fran wasn't thrilled about this, she agreed.

As they entered the office, Larry dropped into a chair and just sat there. The counselor told him that it didn't take a genius to see that he was there against his will, and that they didn't have to talk at all if he didn't want to. But he also suggested that while he was there, Larry might want to hear what the center was all about. The boy relaxed a bit and said that would be okay.

The counselor told him his own story, particularly about his teen years, and then went on to tell him what he thought about homosexuality's roots and why the Bible calls it wrong. Certain parts of the discussion of the roots seemed to hit home. "I have some of those problems," Larry admitted, "but I don't see how they are connected to homosexuality."

As the boy left, the counselor told him that some of the things he'd said were going to come back to him while he was out "messing around," and if he ever decided that he wanted out, he could come back anytime. For the first time, Larry smiled. "Thanks, man. For a Christian, you aren't so bad."

As they entered the waiting room, Fran asked, "Well?"

I looked at Larry and he responded, "Well, he's given me something to think about, anyway."

CHAPTER FIVE

A COUNSELING OUTLINE YOU CAN USE

IT IS GOOD TO REALIZE THAT, WHEN A PERSON COMES TO YOU because of a problem with homosexuality, that is often not *the* problem. Homosexuality is usually only the outward manifestation of the inner root problems. While you may have had little or no experience in counseling homosexuality, you are probably well acquainted with several of the roots such as rejection, bitterness and unforgiveness, self-pity, identity conflicts, etc.

The following outline emphasizes the basic things I try to cover when counseling a person who is struggling with homosexuality. Some of these topics are so fundamental that it is often necessary to return again and again to them as the person both grows in maturity and deals with his or her root problems at deeper and deeper layers.

I. LAYING THE GROUNDWORK

In addition to getting to know a person by taking basic history and hearing what the person wants to say, it is important to establish expectations and understandings in the very beginning. Over the course of counseling, those expectations and understandings may change, so it is also good to check on them from time to time. Initially, however, I ask these questions:

1. What is the nature of your problem?
2. Why have you come for help?
3. Why do you consider it a problem?
4. What is your Biblical perspective on this issue?
5. Do you know anyone else who struggles with this?
   How are his or her struggles the same as yours?
   How are they different?
6. What type of help have you sought before now?
   In what ways did it help?
   In what ways did it fall short?
7. What are your expectations for change?

Not wishing to hear the "gory details," we sometimes have a tendency to overlook inquiring about the true nature of a person's problem. There are varying types of homosexual struggles and degrees of intensity.

Once a young man came to me and confessed that he "fell" homosexually. Neglecting to ask any further questions, I proceeded to counsel him for an hour on how to "pick up the pieces" after a sexual fall. When I finally asked him if the other person knew he was a Christian, he informed me that the other person didn't even know about it. Incredulous, I asked how that could be. He then informed me that his "fall" was looking at a man lustfully from a bus. I had misread him and counseled him for something that hadn't even occurred.

It is also very important to learn what has motivated an individual to come for counseling. While some do come in response to an inner conviction that homosexual behavior is wrong, others come for a variety of other reasons. Some come in response to the demands or urgings of a parent, spouse, or pastor. Some come because of a relationship breakup. Some come because they are feeling society's pressures. Some come because they fear disease. Knowing the reasons can guide you in how (or if) to proceed.

For those who come seeking change, I try to determine how they perceive that change and what unrealistic expectations they might have. A person can't expect help if he announces he has three minutes to give you while you tell him how to become heterosexual. Although this is an extreme example, many do expect to be cured in one session. Such unrealistic expectations need to be dealt with quickly.

It is also important to discover the person's understanding of the Bible's position on homosexuality. There may be an underlying uncertainty as to (a) whether one can change, (b) whether homosexual behavior is sin, (c) or whether God really cares about the person. Any of these, as well as other misconceptions, can greatly hamper further progress. (It is also likely that one little talk will not completely alter the person's perspective.)

When you talk about expectations with a person, it is important that there is a mutual understanding of freedom. What does it mean? When will it come? Why can't the person be free immediately? But the very nature of *life-dominating sins* is that they can't be easily "ordered" away. A common conception of freedom is the absence of temptation. Although this is a non-Biblical belief (see Jas. 1 and I Cor. 10:13), many expect it for those who are ensnared by life-dominating sins like homosexuality.

We expect the alcoholic or the drug addict to never desire a drink or a fix. We expect the homosexual to never be tempted sexually by someone of the same gender. Isn't it odd, though, how easily we excuse recurring problems like laziness, anger, heterosexual lust, or gluttony.

On the other extreme, some think freedom is remaining barely in control. Compared to the bondage they previously experienced, the ability to say "no," no matter how difficult, seems like freedom.

I see freedom as something in between these two extremes. I usually define the goal as "freedom from the *life-dominating effects* of homosexuality." Romans 6:14 says, "For sin shall not be your master," or *have dominion* over you. Sin's dominion over me was more than the surface problem of homosexual behavior. My overt behavior stopped in 1974 when I accepted Jesus as my Lord. But I had to fight it from sunup to sundown. It continued to command my attention, energy, and my emotions as I lived in fear of falling and in feelings of guilt for my past.

For me, *freedom* has been having homosexuality's hold broken over my life in all these areas: behavior, the intensity of temptation (in both quality and quantity), fear, and guilt (both real and false). Freedom has been having life in Jesus be the focus of my attention and identity rather than homosexuality.

Freedom is not the absence of temptations. Temptations fly by from time to time, but there aren't thousands of them playing kamikaze with my mind.

This is realistic freedom; a hope I can honestly offer people. As we comprehend how deep some problems run and how much deeper our relationship with the Lord and one another must run, we will see an increasing number of examples of realized freedom.

II. BURNING THE BRIDGES

Many new believers sincerely desire to have nothing to do with the dominion of darkness but fail to take adequate steps to prevent those forces from seizing them once again. For the most part, those who have maintained their newfound freedom have done so by *burning their bridges*. When we think of the slavery experienced by the Children of Israel in Egypt, it's hard to imagine that they would have ever wanted to go back, but, at times, they did. However, God had "burned the bridge"; the waters of the Red Sea had closed back in. He gave them the gift of making it difficult to go back.

However, helping someone burn bridges is a delicate matter. It tests the person's sincerity in wanting change, but it will also test your gift of discernment. If you take the simplistic approach of pressuring your counselee to "burn" everything without reason or before he or she is truly ready, you will risk destroying your credibility and the relationship.

It is better to suggest and discuss the following areas with the person rather than demand immediate action. If your suggestion is not readily accepted, listen to the counselee's reasons, pray about it, and if you still feel it is indeed a "bridge," bring it up later. After all, bridge burning is a matter of the heart as much as the incinerator.

Bridge 1—Possessions

No one needed to tell me to get rid of my pornography, my occult-oriented books, and my drug-related paraphernalia. I rid myself of these within a few hours after I gave my life to the Lord. My record collection, however, was another matter. As I recall, I purged it in three phases. Category 1 was "definitely evil and must go." This included albums by groups that sang about perversity. Category 2 was "not very bad, but bad for *me*." These were albums by performers who had strong gay followings or whose music elicited memories of gay experiences for me. Category 3 was "not bad, but does it lift me spiritually?" As it turned out, I kept these, but as I became acquainted with Christian music, I seldom listened to them.

I dealt with my books in much the same way. Some were not pornographic, but they dramatized unnatural relationships, both heterosexual and homosexual. For me, at least, they were not good.

Burning this bridge could include love letters or gifts and mementoes from unhealthy relationships.

Bridge 2—Relationships

This is a complicated area for a person to deal with without it coming across as rejecting one's old friends "in the name of

Jesus.'' Those friends have probably experienced enough rejection for a lifetime, and it may have already soured some on Christianity. Nonetheless, the counselee needs to consider his or her strength, which, if the person were truly a homosexual, will not be very strong at this point.

I tried to maintain some of my friendships for a while, but eventually I needed to pull away. I suppose the afternoon that I tried to share Jesus with six of my friends while they were passing some joints around was the day I decided it had gone far enough. In time, when it was clear to me and to them that my life-style had changed, I was able to reestablish contact with a few of them, but only after a time of separation.

I avoided the rejection problem by explaining my newfound spiritual condition and telling them that I needed to devote my time and energies to finding out if this was indeed the truth. I also spoke frankly of the simple logic that parties and old haunts might still be too enticing for a spiritual baby such as myself. Although they felt I was off the track, none of them felt hurt or rejected by my decisions.

Bridge 3—Appearance

For some, the *necessity* of changing their appearance becomes quite an issue. (They're not sure they want to.) For others, the *possibility* of changing their appearance is the major stumbling block. (Will they be able to look more masculine or feminine?) Men and women who have left the homosexual scene may still look like the gay stereotypes, but it is often difficult and confusing to set boundaries in this area. What about jewelry on men? Jeans on women? Long hair? Short hair? Bleached hair? Dyed hair? Makeup? Fingernails? Far-out clothes? Are there any definite rules? I'm afraid not. I find that it's best to approach these questions with a combination of principles and practicality.

The first issue is what a particular appearance means to the individual. A cultivated appearance, especially if it represents a connection to the past, probably needs to go. If it has not been carefully cultivated or has no connection to the past, there may be no harm in it. However, if a man is naturally somewhat effeminate, then flashy clothes or jewelry only add to the problem.

The second concern is what it signifies to others. If one's appearance causes him or her to be ''eyed'' or even solicited when on the street, that's a problem, even if the person doesn't intend to invite that kind of a response. Similarly, if it causes other straight people to label the person or call names, that is a problem because it will work against reinforcing a new identity.

Effeminacy is a particular problem. I feel the word is a misnomer. Many use it to describe the limp wrist, the lisp, and the walks associated with flagrant homosexuals. However, I seldom see a woman carrying herself in these ways. This demeanor seems to be an affectation created in the homosexual world. The pampered, delicate, and fragile look is also a falsely feminine affectation. In these days of health consciousness, most women don't value frailty for themselves, so it's not a truly feminine quality.

Some aspects of so-called effeminacy may be due to the person's natural physique or physical problems. Muscle disorders could lead to a limp wrist. The lisp could be a genuine speech impediment. The delicate and fragile look could be the result of anemia, hemophilia, or some other disease. It would be foolish to try and change these.

On the other hand, the learned aspects of effeminacy can be unlearned. The person who struggles with homosexuality but chooses to make needlepoint his hobby, may defend his pastime by pointing out that Rosey Grier did needlepoint, too. But then Rosey Grier can do just about anything he wants to do without appearing effeminate. This is a relative issue. Some behaviors have been adopted unintentionally, some by a lifetime of modeling oneself after opposite-sex models, and some have been picked up later in life from the homosexual community.

Generally speaking, nagging about effeminacy does not help. The best results are obtained by mentioning the problem and then providing some good role models. Changes in appearance tend to be gradual.

Bridge 4—Memories

For many, memory lane can be far from pleasant. Memories sometimes come like a flood at the unlikeliest times—in church, during prayer or Bible study, or whenever one tries to rest.

Sometimes memories are mere distractions; at other times I believe God may prompt them to remind us of unresolved issues in our lives. Perhaps the counselee still carries hurts or bitterness about a certain person or situation.

In most cases, it is possible to take action on one's memories. One can forgive and be forgiven. One can seriously repent if the memory is about a sinful situation that was earlier excused and swept under the rug. When explicit repentance has occurred, God should be thanked for His forgiveness. One can pray for those who have hurt him or her or whom the person has hurt. (I have found that if it's Satan who is bringing the memory my way, he quits bringing it after I start to seriously pray for the person involved.) As a person begins to deal with troubling memories one at a time, they begin to lose their power to tempt and torment.

Thankfully, the Lord allows people to build new memories with all their new associations. Slowly, those new associations override the old associations and call up new, better memories.

Bridge 5—Identity

Usually, after all the other bridges are burnt and other areas of healing proceed, the bridge of a gay identity begins to go, too. However, there are ways that a person may hinder his or her development of a new identity.

One may look for and associate primarily with others who have come out of the gay background. In moderation, there is a value in this for support and understanding. But, in excess, it can have the effect of prolonging and heightening the old identity. To be identified primarily as an ex-gay places too much emphasis on that background. It separates the person from other Christians and makes the homosexual struggle predominate when there are other sins to struggle against, as well.

Up until this point in the counseling outline, we have been dealing with introductory material and helping a person break away from homosexual *behavior*. If your counselee has been resisting homosexual behavior, that is a major accomplishment, and there should be an acknowledgment of the seriousness of his or her commitment. However, the person may still be under the *dominion* of the sin if the emotional and spiritual conditions which gave rise to it have not been resolved. Remember, homosexuality is usually an ineffective attempt to meet some deeper, legitimate need.

Therefore, to go beyond curtailing the sinful behavior to true freedom from the sin's dominion, we must deal with three more areas: building a sure foundation for the Christian life, healing the hurts from the past, and dealing with other roots of the homosexual problem.

III. BUILDING A SURE FOUNDATION

Individuals struggling with life-dominating sins often live erratic Christian lives. Living by feelings rather than by facts, they become roller coaster Christians. Many wonder if they will ever lead a normal Christian life.

Often these folks have problems with the very foundations of their Christian experience. I have noticed these problems tend to exist in three main areas.

A. Salvation

Many who struggle with homosexuality doubt their basic salvation. Questions such as, "How could God love someone like me?" are common. Some wonder if they have committed the unpardonable sin; others wonder if they are "reprobate" or an "abomination," or they put themselves in some other category which causes them to feel like outcasts. It may have been Christians who insensitively used those names when trying to witness to them in order to convict them of sin.

Also, people may doubt their salvation if they feel no evidence of change. Those who continue to fall into the same sinful behavior and thought patterns may be discouraged. You can help these people fight their feelings of doubt with Scriptural truth found, for example, in Psalm 37:23 and 24: "The steps of a good man are ordered by the Lord: and he delighteth in his way. Though he fall, he shall not be utterly cast down: for the Lord upholdeth him with his hand" (KJV). Good men and women *do* fall but the Lord lifts them up again. Peter walked with the Lord for three years and still denied Him . . . and yet Jesus forgave him. David knew the Lord from his youth and found favor in God's sight, but he was capable of adultery, lying, and murder. And still the Lord lifted him up.

Christians *can want* to sin. It isn't a pleasant truth, but it is still a fact. The Bible acknowledges that there is short-term pleasure in sin (Heb. 11:25). There are times when lying seems more convenient, when blowing up in anger seems more gratifying than forgiving, and when sexual indulgence seems more satisfying than abstinence. In times like these, Christians *can choose* to sin. If the desire to sin didn't continue to plague

Christians, much of the New Testament would be unnecessary. When Peter and Jesus were discussing the issue of forgiveness, Jesus admonished Peter to forgive 70 times seven. Would He ask us to forgive more than He would? Certainly not.

God hates the sin, but He loves the sinner. He's on the sinner's side, anxious to free the person from the thing that enslaves. There is no need for anyone to persist in doubts about his or her salvation. Any person who is unsure about his or her relationship to the Lord can resolve the conflict immediately by praying a sincere sinner's prayer.

B. Relationships

In a very real way, salvation begins several relationships. Most obviously it begins a relationship to God as Father and to Jesus as Redeemer and Brother. But beyond that, salvation also brings one into a family relationship with other Christians. For the homosexual, these relationships can be quite difficult.

The relationship to God can also be difficult for a person striving to leave homosexuality. Christian disciplines like prayer and Bible reading can seem extremely dull to individuals who are accustomed to sensory indulgence. For many, quiet moments are totally foreign. For those folks I suggest the following:

1. *Begin modestly.* Don't try to read the whole Bible or pray around the world. One chapter a day and five or ten minutes of prayer might be a beginning goal.

2. *Background music* (Christian) without words can help some people be still much longer than absolute silence.

3. A *renewed image of God* is necessary for some. If one only can think of God as One who condemns, or if the person's own father was a deficient role model, it may be hard to conceive of God as a loving Father. I frequently suggest that the person spend a few weeks in John 14—17, which personalizes the love of God for us. On a few occasions I have recommended that the person live for a time with a family where there is a father that provides a good model.

Fellowship with other Christians is often difficult. It's hard to love people who might have once condemned you. They may appear so normal and righteous that it is hard for the person newly out of the gay scene to identify with them. And yet there is an important incentive. Broken relationships often clutter the history of homosexuals and provide a root for the problem. It is reasonable to think that good, trustworthy relationships can help with the cure.

C. Double Mindedness

Others who continue to struggle with sins may be caught in the trap of double mindedness by struggling with the following questions:

1. *Is it sin, or isn't it*? While this question persists, the behavior *will* persist. Temptations are hard enough to handle without being weakened in this way.

2. *Can I change, or can't I*? There are many Christians who doubt God's ability to change them and/or their own ability to cooperate with Him in the change process. It is helpful to remember that God said, "You did not choose me, but I chose you . . ." (Jn. 15:16). He knew the difficulties when He called the person, and He decided Christ's blood was sufficient.

3. *Do I want to change, or don't I*? For many this is the bottom-line question. Change is hard and frightening. With life-dominating sins, a person's entire life often revolves around that sin. In coming to God, the person is not in for a minor tune-up but a major overhaul. The best comfort for these fears is a reminder that God knows what's best for the person's life. The Creator is the best re-Creator.

To help clients build a sure foundation I often help them work through these questions:

1. Are you certain that God has forgiven and accepted you? Why or why not?
2. Do you have a good relationship with God?
3. Rank the following in the order of the role they play in your relationship to God: duty, faith, fear, grace, guilt, love, need, other.
4. Describe your relationship with other Christians.
5. What can you do to improve your relationship to other Christians?
6. How would you evaluate homosexuality: as a sin, a problem, or are you uncertain?
7. Do you believe that you can change with God's help?
8. Do you want to change?
9. What factors can lead you to not want to change?

70

IV. HEALING FOR THE PAST

In Chapter 3, I reviewed the research of Elizabeth Moberly and others who suggested that the most common cause of homosexuality was a broken relationship with a parent at a very young age. But how can you find out if this is true for the person you are counseling?

A. Discovering the Origin

1. *Counselee's memory.* In some instances the counselee will be able to tell you. He or she may be able to remember the incident or the situation. He or she may know that months were spent in an incubator, that the parents divorced in the first year, that time was spent in foster homes, etc. However, often this will not be the case. The event will have occurred at too young an age or will have been blocked from conscious memory.

2. *Parental or other reports.* Even if the counselee cannot remember anything traumatic, there may be other significant clues. My mother used to tell me that when I was little I was *inconsolable.* I wouldn't let my parents comfort me when I had been hurt or experienced a loss. A knowledgable counselor might have seen this as what Moberly calls *defensive detachment,* a clue that some time earlier I had been so disappointed in the relationship, that when I was hurting, I wouldn't allow my mother to comfort me for fear that I would be disappointed again. Hospital records or interviews with other family members may provide clues.

3. *Memory.* There have been numerous instances when people have remembered things from their very young childhood. I believe that our prayers have helped them remember things they need to know for healing to take place.

Even if such confirming data is not available, pursuing the theory of parental rejection is usually productive. After all, to a child, the experience that deeply disappoints may seem insignificant and go unnoticed to adults.

B. Breaking the Vow of Detachment

It is important to realize that trauma alone does not cause the defensive detachment described by Moberly. It usually requires the child's decision to defend himself against further hurt by erecting a wall in the relationship: "I'm never going to let you get close enough to me to disappoint or hurt me again."

Prayer for the healing of memories in such situations should contain at least two elements. It should ask the Lord to minister to the initial hurt and heal the pain of it,[1] and it should include an exercise of repentance on the part of the counselee to renounce the vow of detachment. It is hard for us to realize the immense power of negative vows we make in life.

C. Filling the Void

The theory is that from the time of hurt onward, the person contained an internal battle: he or she desperately needed love and relationship with the same-sex parent but was afraid to accept even that which was offered. The person entered adolescence and then adulthood attempting to replace the love and relationship that was missing, and that was the drive to same-sex attachments that became sexual—homosexual. Even then, Moberly, theorizes, if such a relationship began to truly fill the need, the defensive-detachment vow would set in and sabotage the relationship.

But once the decision to detach defensively has been broken, and Jesus heals the original hurt, the person is ready to get on with the growth that was interrupted in the child's development.

The church is the ideal environment in which these "reparative" relationships can happen. In the church there are mature, Christian men and women who can provide the models and love necessary. And they can be clear in their own sexuality so that the relationship does not get off the track and become sexual.

Take this caution seriously. In counseling the person struggling with homosexuality, you are probably the prime candidate for this in-depth kind of relationship. However, if you cannot do the job, make sure that someone else does. I believe that it is absolutely critical in order to achieve freedom from the life-dominating effects of homosexuality.

V. RECKONING WITH THE ROOTS

Guiding a person through this aspect of the counseling outline will likely consume more time than any of the others.

A. Rejection

Rejection for the homosexual seldom ends with an early childhood event. In fact, it is usually just the start of a life of rejection. The defensive detachment may put people off; that may lead to other socially unattractive behaviors, and on the cycle goes, until the child finally concludes he or she *is* different. The first time the child is called queer may have little sexual implication, but the cruelties of childhood peers can take their toll.

I know a man who really had a rough go of it as a kid. He had two strikes against him in his neighborhood. For one thing, there was a rumor that continued to go around that his father wasn't really his father. People said that during his parents' engagement, his mother had slept with another man. The other thing was that he was a "goody-goody." He just wouldn't take part in fighting, name-calling, or picking on the little kids. He wouldn't listen to dirty jokes, and he never once talked back to his father. A lot of times he stayed home to do his homework. Naturally, the other kids thought he was a little odd. And they let him know it. But the seed of rejection did not take root. His name was Jesus. The Bible tells us that "He was despised and rejected by men" (Isa. 53:3), but it didn't cause Him to withdraw or respond with bitterness.

Unfortunately, that is not the case with many. Feelings of rejection by those who matter most—first family, then friends at school and maybe even church, and eventually society—cause many to shrink back, nurse the hurts, and ask "why?" Too often the answer is (a) *"I'm* a creep," and (b) *"They're all* creeps."

What are the steps out of this dead-end street?

1. Help the individual recognize those attitudes of rejection toward himself or herself and others, including the line that says, "Reject them before they reject you." (Notice how similar this is to the defensive detachment a small child might focus on a parent.)

2. In prayer, help the person tell God that he or she consciously turns from this way of thinking. Have the person pray that God will give him or her His perspective on both self and others.

3. Finally, it is important that you work with the people in your church so that this person will be able to experience new relationships of acceptance in the Body of Christ. Realizing that God's people love him or her will be very important in believing that God loves the person, too.

B. Rebellion

Rebellion has subtle dynamics. Its effect on a Christian's life can be devastating if not caught. Saying "no" to God in one area can lead to rebellion in other areas.

For the Christian who struggles with homosexuality, it can be the ultimate weapon for getting his or her way, or rather it can seem like that to the person. When others let the person down, or even when God does not "cooperate" with the person's wishes, he or she may be tempted to take revenge by destroying all that God has done and making futile all the time others have invested in his or her life.

Through the root of rebellion comes one of the greatest temptations to new homosexual behavior. Of course, lesser levels of rebellion can occur, too, like not being very cooperative with new steps of growth.

Whether an individual is conscious or not of the rebellion, turning away from God and His will is always sin, regardless of how it manifests itself. Confession and repentance is in order for recognized rebellion.

C. Fear

Until a few years ago, fear had had a tight grip on me, and it usually plagues others struggling with homosexuality. Without any cause I was aware of, I used to fear that my parents would leave me somewhere when they went away. Older kids would tease me with threats that monsters were going to get me. Some kids seem able to laugh that kind of thing off, but not me. I carried it for weeks, even years.

As I grew up, the focus of my fear changed direction, but I continued to fear the unknown. I feared failure. And I also feared *change*.

Imagine a person who has spent an entire lifetime thinking, "I am different." Picture that person finally finding an identity, a place where he or she fits in, is accepted and feels secure. Realize that this identity revolves around a sinful life-style, and then you can imagine how conversion to Christ challenges everything important to that person. It means facing the unknown, risking failure, and undergoing radical change.

One way of dealing with fear is to find security in Jesus as that "someone bigger and stronger." Another way is to focus on His character, His strength, and His love, and allow His perfect love to cast out all fear. Of course, one needs to practice doing these things. They won't happen all at once. For me, singing Scripture songs, as well as meditating on passages like Psalm 27; Joshua 1:9; and Isaiah 43:1-3, played important roles.

D. Self-Pity

Self-pity has long been an effective tool of the enemy for rendering God's people helpless. In I Kings 19:14, the prophet is whining and complaining with self-pity. He moans, "I am the only one left" (who has remained faithful).

Elijah had just finished challenging 450 prophets of Baal concerning whose god was greater. He stood alone taunting and mocking their god. He witnessed the power of the Lord as the heavens opened and rained down fire in answer to Elijah's prayer.

What had happened? The circumstances had not changed. He had challenged the prophets of Baal alone. No one supported him then, and yet he remained steady, trusting entirely in the Lord.

The only thing that had changed him from a powerful prophet to a pouting one was a shift in focus—from the all-powerful God to the all-too-human prophet. Whereas God was equal to the challenge, the prophet, in himself, was not.

Elijah's predicament reveals some vital information about self-pity. First, self-pity is usually a *very subtle* change in focus from Jesus to ourselves. Second, self-pity obscures the truth. (God had to reveal to Elijah that there were actually 7,000 who remained faithful.) Third, it can happen to anybody.

In my experience, self-pity has been a large attitudinal perspective for the majority of those coming out of the gay lifestyle. So how does one break out of such a crippling habit?

Helping the person you are counseling to know the enemy is half the battle, and in that regard, I suggest three things. (a) It is essential to see self-pity as a sin in itself. It is not an attitude that can be pampered or tolerated in our lives. A little indulgence will lead one deeper into self-indulgence. So repentance is key. (b) It is important for the person to become open to members of the Body of Christ and invite them to point out when they see self-pity. You as a counselor won't be there all the time; others must assist, and the counselee must be willing to accept the warnings. (c) There should be regular prayer for wisdom and spiritual discernment in order to spot and reject untruths and discover the promises and purposes of God.

E. Envy

Very early in my counseling with a person struggling with homosexuality I ask two questions: "What kind of a same-sex partner do you find attractive?" and "If you could change anything about yourself, what kind of a person would you like to be?" In the majority of situations, the answers to both questions are nearly identical.

A guy who admits to preferring men of a certain physical stature usually wishes that he could look like that. Someone who is searching for a man who "has his head together" will often admit that he is lacking in stability. A man or woman who falls far short of society's standards for masculinity or femininity will often search for a "real man" or a "take-charge woman" as a sexual partner. Many who admit to a strong genital fixation will also admit that they feel inferior in their own genital endowment. Those who are growing older often look for youth and innocence.

In counseling a young homosexual, Leanne Payne asked, "Do you know anything at all about the habits of cannibals? Do you know *why* they eat people?" The young person admitted he didn't, and so Payne answered, "Cannibals eat only those they admire, and they eat them *to get their traits*."[2] The same motivation subconsciously drives many homosexuals as they strive to possess the manhood or womanhood they feel they don't have.

Galatians 5:21 warns that those who envy will not inherit the Kingdom of God. It calls for direct confession and repentance. Many who have repented time and time again for lust find that if they include repentance for the sin of envy, they begin to make progress in resisting the temptations. Finally, it is important to realize that God doesn't measure us by worldly standards. God looks at the heart, not one's physical stature. The fruit of the Spirit is the thing to strive for, not for a different body.

F. Bitterness

Bitterness causes everyone trouble.

Women have come into our office desiring to break from lesbianism, but they bring an unwillingness to release bitterness toward one or more individuals, usually men. Often unresolved bitterness over incest, rape, or some other kind of abuse is at the bottom of their leanings toward homosexuality. And it's often the tool Satan uses to keep them there.

Men come for counseling about impossible standards their fathers set for them. Some have bitterness over the fact that their fathers never seemed to care. Others are bitter toward a society that did not tolerate variations from its definitions of masculinity. They are often bitter over sexual abuse by a father, brother, or older kid in the neighborhood.

Anger is an understandable response to these tragic occurrences, but we are also admonished to forgive. Our anger cannot be an excuse for hatred. Ephesians 4:26 advises, "In your anger do not sin: Do not let the sun go down while you are still angry, and do not give the devil a foothold." Many times the cycle of anger into bitterness results in self-hate that the person didn't do or say anything. Then self-esteem goes down, false guilt enters, then self-pity, and soon all defenses against sexual misbehavior disappear.

G. Deception

There are many excuses that a person can believe about himself or herself that will ensnare the person in homosexuality. For example, "I've been different for as long as I can remember. Isn't that proof that I was born gay?" or "I saw some gay pornography, and it made something stir in me. That's when I realized that I was sexually interested in my own sex," or "I have had lots of heterosexual experiences, but I've never really felt completely fulfilled." The list could go on forever.

As a counselor, your job is to point out the falsehood in these attitudes and feelings. Many early assumptions gays make about their own homosexuality are based totally in the ignorance of adolescence. Some are propaganda accepted from the gay community. Some can even be misinterpretations of Scripture.

Your own experience, the resource of the Bible, and many of the ideas covered elsewhere in this book should help you shine light on the deceptions.

H. Moral Impurity

Sexual stimulation bombards the senses of most Americans daily. Whether heterosexual or homosexual in nature, it can lead to moral impurity in the mind of the individual. How does one wage war on an enemy that seems to have people surrounded?

The first step is to break every association with moral impurity by reducing the stimulation to illicit sex. This means pornography and borderline pornography and any literature that glorifies sexual sin, regardless of its homosexual or heterosexual orientation. It also means avoiding questionable television shows and movies. The person should even avoid stores where soft pornography is on display. It may mean avoiding the beach or other places where people dress scantily. If the person has a problem with mentally undressing people, suggest that they pray for the person whenever they are tempted.

A second step is to fill the mental "void" with positive things. Philippians 4:8 says, "Finally, brothers, whatever is true, whatever is noble, whatever is right, whatever is pure, whatever is lovely, whatever is admirable—if anything is excellent or praiseworthy—think about such things."

A third step is to fill one's life with Christian fellowship and service.[3] Idleness is not helpful for the person trying to resist moral impurity, and the Bible says that we need the Body of Christ. It also says that two are better than one, because if one falls, the other one can pick him up (Eccl. 4:9, 10).

I. Oppression

Oppression is a term that has come into common use in some Christian circles, and its meaning connotes spiritual bondage or a heavy dose of demonic buffeting on a Christian.

I've seen a lot of emotional and spiritual damage done to individuals who were told that a deliverance session would solve all their problems. As a result, I tend to be very cautious about dealing on the level of Satanic influence. For those who have been involved in occult practices, there is the strong possibility that they've left themselves open to demonic influences.

Occult involvement can be much broader than the dramatic experiences of seances or black Sabbaths. Any efforts to obtain supernatural guidance, power, or advantage through a source other than God is an occult activity.

Although the root of oppression can run deep, it is no more difficult to deal with than other roots. It's my conviction that any door to the occult that has been willfully *or* unknowingly opened in a person's life has to be deliberately shut. A specific and conscious repentance and renunciation of the influence and activity is the way to close the door.

In looking at oppression from this angle, however, I am still not ruling out the importance of discipleship and obedience to God's Word. And I am also not ruling out the possibility, in fact the probability, that such a person has other roots as well for their homosexual struggles. It's seldom that Satan does not play upon an existing weakness in a person's life.

CHAPTER SIX

HOW TO ENLIGHTEN
YOUR CHURCH

THE CHURCH IS DESIGNED TO BE THE PRIMARY ENVI-
ronment for ministry and nurture even—and especially—to
people struggling with homosexuality. Some churches and
many Christians have difficulty providing the help that is needed. How can we develop and share compassion, commitment,
confidence in the person's ability to change, and upgrade our
competency in guiding change?

Nowhere is this need more fully illustrated than in the story of
Perry Desmond, a transsexual who ran an occult shop on Bour-
bon Street in New Orleans. Almost daily, Christians barraged the
French Quarter with tracts. Perry had received many. One day
the truth hit home, and Perry realized his need for the Lord. The
following Sunday he showed up in the church from which the
ministry teams had originated. Since he no longer owned any
male clothing, he dressed in his regular female attire. But the
church was not ready to receive him. (Some claim that was the
first time the church failed to give an altar call to join the
church.) Although this is an extreme example, it illustrates how
unprepared our churches are to minister in this area.

As I was growing up, the young people in my church were
quite often frustrated with me. I acted different than they did; I
looked different; I used words they were unfamiliar with; and I
was more needy than most. Fortunately, what they lacked in
confidence and competence they made up for in compassion and
commitment. One elder instructed them that "love is not an
option for Christians; it is a command. I know Ed's difficult to
deal with, but you just have to keep on loving him. It's the only
way he's ever going to change." So they did and so I have.

My personal experience is unique in that I "survived" without
any professional or pastoral counseling. The help that I received
came from my peers, my fellow Christians. None of them had
any special training in homosexuality or in any kind of counseling. Their major qualification was simply that they believed in

God and in His desire to set me free. They made themselves available on that basis.

I still recall most of their simple, yet practical, advice, after I came to the Lord. My cousin, a fairly young Christian herself, told me, "Look, Ed, the Bible says that Jesus came that you might have life and have it more abundantly. Now, I don't know how He plans to work that out in your life. I don't know anyone else who used to be gay. But I've got to believe that He can do it. I'm willing to stick with you until we see that happen." She didn't make it sound like it would be easy, but I knew she was going to be there. She didn't suggest magical solutions, but what she did say almost made it sound like an adventure.

Another friend who had been a Christian for a few years advised me, "Look, I know they always tell a new Christian to read the Gospel of John, but I think that you should read James first. James is all about temptation, and if you don't learn how to deal with temptation, I'm afraid you might not stick around long enough to make it through John."

My first major breakthrough came with some counsel I received from my first Christian roommate, less than a year old in his faith. I was greatly discouraged about feelings of homosexual lust that I was having toward guys in our church, and even the assistant pastor. His response astounded me: "So you lust after the assistant pastor, do you? So what! I lust after the pastor's daughter. Yeah, that doesn't make it right, but let's face facts. Less than a year ago, we were both on the streets. Some things don't change overnight. We've *got* to stick with the church 'cause that's where the change is gonna happen."

As our discussion continued, Jimmy helped me see that my struggles were *just the same* as his; they only pursued a different object. Suddenly, the Bible opened up for me. The verses on temptation and overcoming were for me, too!

Another incident occurred in my second year of Bible school. I was having a major struggle with homosexual lust and my usual counselors were off on a ministry trip. Not knowing what else to do, I finally asked my ex-football player roommate to wear more than just his underwear around the apartment because I was having some struggles. I thought maybe he'd hit me or go for the dean. Instead, he looked at me and said, "I bet you're kicking yourself because you're having these temptations. But I've thought about it, and . . . if I were living in the girls' dorm with my past sin running around in front of me in bra and panties, I'd have fallen long ago. You've been here for two years and this is the first time you've had a problem with it. That's pretty good. Brother, it looks to me like you've come a long way, and you ought to be rejoicing instead of whining. Change takes time.''

Two common threads in all this advice were "have patience" and "isn't that just like my struggle?" Nothing new and earth-shattering. Just plain, simple, *practical* counsel. When we stop treating homosexuality as a special problem, we realize that it is a sin *like any other*. If we can communicate this message to the people in the pews, effective ministry will follow.

In order for the church to minister to homosexuals, the church needs to deal with the following areas:

Confronting Hypocrisy

The knowledge that all of our sins have similar roots could have major ramifications in the church. This knowledge could silence the hypocrite who takes delight in believing that his or her sins are somehow less serious than the homosexual's sins. The Bible says even our righteousness is as filthy rags! It's ludicrous to hold onto a sin-meter mentality where we rank our sins on a scale of one to ten.

Confronting Homophobia

This knowledge could also confront homophobia (the fear of homosexuals). Many times that fear is based on ignorance. We don't know who they are or where they come from. We hold onto these dark and sinister images. When we realize that they are people like us who come from our own families and churches, the homophobia often dissipates. Information throughout this book will give you a better picture. Pick what you feel would best fit the needs of your group.

Encouraging Evangelism

I still recall my early days as a street ministry leader. In the first month of Bible school, my testimony leaked out, and I was asked to lead a group going to the gay bars of Dallas. On our first ministry outing, nearly 60 students showed up. Among them were a few guys who I perceived to be "red-neck queer bashers." Before we left, I took them aside and asked them why they were there. One of them replied, "Ed, I'm ashamed to admit it, but we used to beat up gays. Now that we know you and we know more about what they really struggle with, well, we want to make it up somehow. We want to let them know that Jesus loves them, too.'' Even now, that memory brings chills to my spine. These guys ended up being the most effective and faithful evangelists on my team.

Confronting Complacency

This type of knowledge also confronts complacency. It is easy to feel nothing for the sinner "out there"—the one who lurks in some dark corner of the city. But when we realize that that person is someone's son or daughter, or is someone who works with us, lives next door, or attends our church, the complacency often disappears.

Confronting Cheap Grace

The knowledge that some are, in fact, changing, and recognizing that their sin struggle is similar to our own also challenges the permissive attitudes toward homosexuality. Permissiveness masquerades as compassion, but it is far from it. Is it compassionate to pretend that alcoholism is not a problem? Would it be compassionate to tell a compulsive liar or overeater that there is nothing wrong with his or her behavior? Certainly change is difficult, but compassion cannot ignore the destructiveness of the behavior—if not physically and emotionally, at least spiritually.

Dealing with the Aftermath

Two areas of heightened concern recently are the political issues and the AIDS epidemic. These may need to be confronted directly, if and when they appear. As Christians, I believe that it is sound practice for our expressions of love to always precede our political and social concerns.

In many ways, the expression of our Gospel message validates our political concerns. For example, can we protest the wickedness of the media without proposing some wholesome alternatives? Unfortunately, we can and we have, but the world looks on in wonder. We ought not make statements against the evils of homosexuality until we have presented a message of hope and redemption to those caught in its snare. We need to be part of the solution.

Dealing with Homosexual Sin in the Church

For the most part, we have been assuming that individuals in the church who have this problem are, basically, repentant. Unfortunately, two unpleasant truths remain. One is that even repentant people can fall. The other is that not all church members are repentant. Either way, the repercussions from sexual falling can have a profound effect on a church.

Quite often, the way a homosexual problem is uncovered in a church is through a sexual fall. Sometimes, the individual comes to the pastor to confess the fall and to ask for counsel. These situations, naturally, are easier to deal with.

Lead Them Not into Temptation

Many of our clients are contending with a variety of emotional and spiritual problems, and consequently may continue to fall sexually even months after counseling has begun. Our role is a ministry of reconciliation—leading them to a place of repentance and attempting to discover what weaknesses may have led to the fall, so that we can counsel them in those areas. Very often, in an instance of homosexual falling, the issue is not lust but another emotional problem. Some respond sexually to loneliness or feelings of rejection. Some have had lifelong patterns of using sex to appease feelings of stress or depression. While these do not excuse the sexual behavior, they do help to explain it and serve as a guideline for future counseling.

I am aware of times when the sexual fall has been the direct result of what could only be described as a snare. One Bible school dean relayed a situation where roommates were selected at random. In a three-person, one-bedroom apartment, three former homosexuals "happened" to end up as roommates. The odds against this are astronomical and yet it happened. Two of the young men fell in a weak moment and the third walked in and discovered them. At this writing, only one of them has survived spiritually.

Early in my Christian walk I began to feel that the people in my church could only see my faults and recognized none of their own. With self-pity I felt that no one really loved me. As I stood on the corner waiting for a bus that would not come, a young, attractive man (what I now call a "tailor-made temptation") began flirting with me. For nearly 20 minutes I played the cat-and-mouse game before I suddenly wondered, "Why is this young hunk suddenly throwing himself at me now, when this type of thing never happened to me before?'' The enemy of our souls does play against our weaknesses and bruises. If I had given in, I hope that would not have marked the end of my Christian experience or my involvement with my church.

I do not believe that sin will destroy a church if it is dealt with lovingly and in repentance; it is unrepented sin that eats at a church like cancer. But as loving brothers and sisters we need to be alert to the needs of and and temptations facing weaker Christians and do everything possible to cause them not to stumble.

There are no easy answers for dealing with sexual sin. I tend to view each situation differently. Some people stumble into sin; some fall; some play around on the edges until they fall in; and others jump. My first response to the news of a sexual fall is, ''What *really* happened?''

Church Discipline

God's response to sin is chastisement. That chastisement is designed to lead us to reconciliation. Consider David's sin with Bathsheba. It may have started as a snare. (David was not looking for that first peek at Bathsheba bathing.) But then David began to conspire and engineer the circumstances so that he could have sex with her. God's response included chastisement. His discipline included teaching and correction. We must be careful that we follow God's pattern. All too often our discipline means only punishment.

What About 'Exposing the Sin'?

In dealing with homosexuality, another popular method of discipline—i.e., ''exposing the sin before the church''—is also counterproductive. In most cases, the individual usually leaves the church immediately. The stigma attached to homosexuality is so severe that most individuals cannot live with the results of the exposure. And according to Matthew 18:15-19, the whole church is to be informed only if the person has rejected the concern of a few brothers or sisters *brought in private*. Reconciliation is the goal, and this method ought to be considered only as the last resort.

The Real Goal: Reconciliation

With reconciliation as an ultimate goal, I have learned of several situations that have worked. In one situation involving a leader, the sexual fall had become known to a number of people and the integrity of the ministry was at stake. But public exposure was curtailed. The only thing that was revealed was that the leader had some serious problems that needed to be dealt with, and he was being relieved of his responsibilities so that he could seek help for his problem. In this case, love covered the exact nature of the sin, but still reckoned with it.

In another instance, a congregation member who was repeatedly falling sexually was warned that exposure *might* result (used as an incentive), and he was required to meet weekly with the pastor and, occasionally, with me. The accountability and counsel enabled him to deal with his problems, and the issue was never made public.

What About Unrepentance?

The Biblical guidelines for dealing with unrepentance, detailed in Matthew 18 and I Corinthians 5, are quite clear. It is in these circumstances that "disfellowshipping" is called for. It should be noted that, even in these instances, the ultimate goal is twofold: so that the "yeast" will not work through "the whole batch of dough," *and* that the individual's soul might be saved. Just as a parent ought not to discipline a child in anger, the church ought not to discipline in this way if *both* goals are not in their hearts. It is not only to rid the church of sin, but also to help the individual recognize his folly and, one day, repent. And this can happen.

For instance, while I was in college and before I gave my life to the Lord, I had a brief encounter with Christianity but went back to drugs and the gay life. (This was not the time when I made a vow with the Lord to "come back when I am on top.") However, after returning to my sinful life, I maintained contact with some friends from the college Christian fellowship. In some ways, I was enjoying the best of both worlds. I had my fun and pleasure, but when I was depressed, I could go to my Christian friends.

One day I got a letter from Joe, my closest Christian friend. On the outside were the words to a song: "If you find out where you're going, let me know; I love you just enough to let you go.'' Inside, my friend attempted to explain what he was doing. In a fit of anger I threw the letter across the room. ''If that's what Christians are,'' I said, ''I want no part of them.'' Still, my friend succeeded in showing me that I couldn't ride in on his coattails; I was living a different life and was separated from the benefits of Christianity.

The best part of this story comes with my eventual surrender to the Lord in 1974. When I told one of my old Christian friends about it, she literally screamed with joy. ''Have you called Joe?'' she asked. ''He has this little card on his desk that says, 'Pray for Ed.' He never forgot you.''

This is discipline with reconciliation as a goal.

AN OUTLINE FOR SERVICE

In the task of educating the church, you will need to draw on all the material included in this book. Some should be presented from the pulpit. Some should be shared with the leaders and teachers in the church so that they can deal more sensitively with people struggling with homosexuality. Parents and close friends will need personal counseling to deal with their feelings of guilt and ways of relating. But who should hear what?

I. The Whole Congregation

Sermons and other communications, such as a column in the church bulletin or newsletter, are times when general information should be passed on. However, homosexual issues should not become a crusade greater than any other concern. In those public contexts, I recommend addressing the following:

1. *Theology*—what the Bible says. Be sure to put the sinful aspects of homosexuality in context and communicate hope.

2. *The situation*. Occasionally it is appropriate to note the pervasiveness of homosexual struggles. Those struggling won't feel so alone, and it may reduce some head-in-the-sand attitudes among others.

3. *Homophobia*. The fear of homosexuals, of ''catching'' homosexuality, and the fear of AIDS severely hinders love. The pulpit is a good place to address these fears.

4. *Unconditional love*. Separating the sinner from the sin, underscoring God's love and power, and understanding our universal sinful history is all important in communicating hope to the person struggling with homosexuality and love from those not troubled by that sin.

II. Leaders and Teachers

In addition to the public teaching to guide your church, there may be times when it is necessary to work directly with certain leadership people. Some may be teachers or leaders in groups where participants struggle with homosexuality. Some may be on boards or committees where decisions affecting funding or policy relevant to ministry to homosexuals is determined. Some may have an inappropriate, personal intolerance toward the gay person. For these leaders and teachers, you may want to schedule a retreat or some other occasion to address the following:

1. *Sensitivity.* Greater sensitivity to what constitutes clear but inoffensive teaching may be needed. That is, greater effort should be put into clearly stating that homosexual behavior is *wrong, forgivable,* and *healable,* without demeaning those people who struggle with it.

2. *Understanding* something of the roots of homosexuality may be important for those in positions where they would be counseling families (where bad parent-child dynamics might stimulate homosexuality), running day-care centers, or directly befriending and ministering to people struggling with homosexuality.

3. *Wisdom* will certainly be needed among the leaders if the church must consider various levels of discipline for persistent sin.

4. *Thwarting rejection.* Frequently teachers and youth leaders will notice that some child is being rejected or ridiculed by his or her peers. Teaching (and in some cases, requiring) love and tolerance within the Christian community is a responsibility of the leaders. We must do everything possible to ensure that no child in the Christian community is "pushed" into concluding that he or she is homosexual simply because of other differences.

III. Family

Family members of a person with a history of homosexuality need all the above in even greater measure. Plus they need help with the following:

1. *Guilt.* No question is greater for parents and sometimes siblings than "why?" Sometimes there are causes like a lack of love, an unnecessary separation, sexual abuse and incest. Whenever these kinds of things surface, the Christian Gospel of repentance and God's forgiveness is absolutely essential. Apologies to and forgiveness from the offended party are also important for reconciliation and healing. If the whole family is within the context of the church, this is the *most* hopeful, though delicate, situation.

2. *Relief from false guilt.* Sometimes no causes can be found and still parents agonize over what they did wrong. They need help to see that our God-given free will allows anyone (even their children) to make wrong choices with no one else to blame.

3. *Help against bitterness.* Anger and resentment are also frequent emotions for family members as they wonder "why is he doing this to us?" They may feel great embarrassment and disappointment.

4. *Support not to separate.* All these emotions provide a great temptation to withdraw from the person struggling with homosexuality. Supporting these parents and family members in their pain and helping them remain loving toward the gay person is a role that the church can fulfill.

When You're Over Your Head

What happens if you get in over your head helping a homosexual? It can happen. You may hit a situation that you are not emotionally ready to handle, or perhaps you realize that you don't have the training you need to deal with a particular problem. Or perhaps the person is a close family member or friend.

Trust your feelings here. Be open to talking about your frustrations with a trained Christian counselor. There is no shame in admitting, for example, that you can't deal with some particularly unsavory details.

In addition to many, many trained Christian counselors, there are organizations available to be the helper's helper. A ministry network is mentioned in the last chapter of this book: EXODUS. Call the phone number and find out if there are chapters in your area. (Chapters are located across the country near most large cities.) This organization is built on a Christian base. Chapters will differ according to the local leadership, so you may want to carefully question local leaders—either about specific areas you would like help on, or about directly dealing with the counselee.

Remain the counselee's friend. Let the person know that you care deeply and you will be praying. Explain why you are asking others for outside help.

CHAPTER SEVEN

ANSWERS TO THE QUESTIONS PEOPLE ASK

T HIS CHAPTER SHOULD NOT BE USED IN PLACE OF A CAREFUL study of the other principles in this book. But when counseling with people, one often finds that some specific question stands in their way of progress. There are also a number of questions that are too unique to be covered by the deeper discussions. Therefore, this chapter is provided for your help.

Questions Homosexuals Ask

1. *Wasn't I born this way?*
The causes of homosexuality may stem from disrupted parental relationships in earliest infancy, but there is no clinical evidence of persons being born homosexual. In his *Textbook for Psychosexual Disorders*, Clifford Allen categorically states, "No investigations in any sphere indicate an organic basis for homosexuality, whether physical, chemical, cellular, microscopic or macroscopic."[1]

As a Christian who accepts the complete change that Christ offers through salvation, I accept this position. In addition, the Bible mentions homosexuality as sin and therefore a condition that Christ died to cure.

2. *How do you explain the fact that I've had these feelings since I was a child?*
Which came first, the feelings of being different or an explicitly sexual attraction for the same sex? Many have come to the conclusion that they are gay simply because society was intolerant of their uniqueness. Since they didn't measure up to society's stereotypes of maleness or femaleness, they *assumed* they must fit into another category. It is also reasonable that if the cause of a person's homosexuality was a disrupted relationship with one of his or her parents at a very young age, then the driving need to repair that relationship would have been felt from that early age.

91

3. *Will I have to become straight?*
First, one needs to define straight. Much of what we commonly call straight is still pretty crooked by God's definition. Many straights, for example, are involved in sex outside of marriage (what God calls fornication). By straight, we also don't mean an "all-American boy" who guzzles beer while watching TV and lives for his car. These are stereotypes. As your Creator, God has a plan for your maleness (or femaleness). Yes, if you intend to grow in your Christian life, you will have to become straight—working at making Christ's image in your life more and more clear as you mature in your faith.

4. *Will I have to get married?*
Not necessarily. It seems to be God's purpose that some people remain single. Paul even encouraged a single life-style. In any event, the decision to marry or to remain single ought to be a *free* choice, coming from a place of strength rather than weakness, i.e., you shouldn't get married to get "healed" and you shouldn't remain in a place where you *can't* get married due to fears, phobias, or aversions to the opposite sex.

5. *Why are you picking on homosexuality?*
We are not picking on homosexuality. We address all sin in much the same way. It is our desire to extend to the homosexual the same Gospel message that we would extend to any other sinner. The good news is that, although you are caught in sin, there is a way out, a way of hope and redemption in Jesus Christ.

6. *Is homosexual behavior the unpardonable sin?*
Homosexual behavior is not the unpardonable sin. The issue of the unpardonable sin is mentioned twice in the Bible; both instances are worded very much the same. In Matthew 12:31 and Mark 3:29 the unpardonable sin is blasphemy against the Holy Spirit, not homosexual behavior. Also, in I Corinthians 6:11 Paul mentions homosexuals along with other sinners, but then he says, "And that is what some of you were. But you were washed, you were sanctified, you were justified in the name of the Lord Jesus Christ and by the Spirit of our God." Clearly, full pardon is available for the homosexual.

7. *What about my basic orientation?*

Orientation is a peculiar word. It seems that we have borrowed it from psychology only in this area. If we spoke about your lying, selfishness, or sin orientation, would you expect those to totally go away? It's the same with homosexuality. With God's help, your temptations will decrease in both intensity and frequency, but you may face occasional temptations throughout your lifetime.

8. *When will I lust after the opposite sex?*
It isn't God's plan to lead you out of one lust into another. The process of change first involves an unlearning of the homosexual condition, and then a learning or relearning of the heterosexual one. It is important to realize that much of what passes as normal heterosexual drive and desire is also fallen.

9. *Do I have to give up my gay friends?*
Many new believers sincerely desire to have nothing to do with the dominion of darkness but fail to take adequate steps to prevent those forces from seizing them once again. For the most part, those who have maintained their newfound freedom have done so by burning old bridges behind them. When we think of the slavery experienced by the Children of Israel in Egypt, it's hard to imagine that they would have ever wanted to go back, but, at times, they did. However, God had "burned the bridge"; the waters across the Red Sea had closed back in. Recognizing your spiritual babyhood will help you see that you'll need all the help you can get. Knowing you can't go back may be essential. However, there are ways of breaking off old relationships that do not automatically give a rejection message.

10. *Do I have to give up my music, etc.?*
This is also part of burning the bridges (mentioned in the previous question). For the most part, music, books, clothes, appearance, and anything else associated with the gay life-style may need to go. Often it depends on what that possession means to you and whether it links you to your old life. This is a time of choice between freedom and the pleasures of sin.

11. *Will reading* Playboy *help?*
Reading *Playboy* and other similar magazines will only create other problems. It may lead to lust, fragmented attraction,

repulsions, etc. The philosophy of *Playboy* and other "girlie" magazines, let alone more hard-core pornography, portrays women as objects, encourages promiscuity, and is as un-Christian as homosexuality.

12. *What about David and Jonathan or Jesus and John in the Bible? Were these homosexual relationships?*
No. Those are not logical assumptions. David, although he loved Bathsheba, eventually repented for his sin with her because it went against God's Law. If he had been sexually involved with Jonathan, why didn't he repent of that, too?

If Jesus and John were lovers, why didn't John object to Paul listing homosexuality as a sin in I Corinthians 6:9-11 and I Timothy 1:9-11?

13. *I've heard of homosexual marriages that have lasted five or ten years. Doesn't that indicate it is a successful option?*
Length has nothing to do with success. A heterosexual marriage that lasts only that long is said to end in failure. Furthermore, the large majority of homosexuals make little effort at monogamous relationships, some even having hundreds of partners. Even in the gay church where monogamy is espoused, there is often a different standard than the Biblical heterosexual standard. For instance, the gay church doesn't seem to object to sex before marriage or serial marriages (i.e., monogamy for a time and then a new "monogamous" relationship).

I do not believe homosexual behavior under any rationalization is acceptable.

Questions the Church Asks
1. *Is homosexuality caused by a demon?*
It seems that homosexuality is no more demonic than any other sin condition. Though it is true that all sin is to some degree Satanically inspired, the tendency to view homosexuality as uniquely demonic is troubling. In some instances a demon may be involved, but that should not be the prime presumption. One danger in assuming demonic involvement is to overlook the usually long process of healing and growth that is needed for recovery from homosexuality. A person may think exorcism should solve it all and then become more confused and discouraged when temptation or even a fall follows. If a long road of

growth is not expected, the person is just set up for disillusionment. Disillusionment destroys hope, and without hope people give up.

2. *Isn't homosexuality the worst sin?*
In Romans 1:24-27 homosexual behavior is clearly described as sinful and part of the moral bankruptcy of the pagan world. However, in Chapter 2, Paul points out that the Jews were just as bankrupt, even though they had the Law, because they were hypocrites. Romans 3:10-12 concludes, "There is no one righteous, not even one; there is no one who understands, no one who seeks God. All have turned away, they have together become worthless; there is no one who does good, not even one." Also, in I Corinthians 6:9-11 and I Timothy 1:9-11, homosexual behavior is mentioned in the middle of lists of other sins, with nothing to distinguish it as being the *worst* one.

3. *Can a person be a gay Christian?*
Yes, but not for long. First of all, we need to realize that we don't clean up our act and then become a Christian; we become a Christian and then receive both the power and the conviction to clean up our act. While ridding the sinner of homosexual behavior (and other "action" sins) might be *our* priority, God often starts by dealing with underlying issues like rejection and takes care of the homosexual problem later. (As a pastor you might reflect on whether *you* have had any sin in your life that God didn't free you of right away.)

4. *Isn't becoming a homosexual a choice people make?*
Yes, but a limited one. Some people may make a rather conscious choice to get involved in sexually bizarre activities and finally choose homosexuality. But it is more typical for a person to conclude that he or she is homosexual by the age of 11 to 13. Often the young person may feel that he or she is homosexual through no choice of his or her own. We shouldn't use words like "choice" to condemn people.

5. *Can a 'regular' Christian help?*
Definitely yes. Being a friend, offering good models of loving Christian maturity, are all essential for the recovery of the Christian struggling with homosexuality. Some may be able to

provide that deep kind of relationship so essential in meeting the person's unmet childhood needs. This doesn't require a trained counselor. It just requires someone who is secure in his or her own sexuality and is willing to make the necessarily deep relational commitment.

6. *How do I evangelize homosexuals?*
Just like anybody else. The issue isn't homosexuality; it's their need for Jesus. You could clean up their homosexual problems, and they'd still be without Jesus. Evangelize like you'd evangelize anyone else, and let *them* bring up homosexuality as an issue.

7. *Are homosexuals safe around children?*
The answer is not a simple yes or no. The answer depends on the individual, homosexual or heterosexual. Because molestation *is* a serious problem in our society, adults responsible for children should take reasonable measures to teach all children the difference between "good touch" (a friendly hug) and "bad touch" (touching private parts or against one's will), and other safety measures. It's also important to *listen* if a child expresses discomfort or fear around certain adults or older children.

8. *How will I know a homosexual?*
Many times you won't. Most people who say they can spot a homosexual really mean that they can spot the stereotype. Many people who fit the stereotype are not gay; many people who are gay do not fit the stereotype.

9. *What about that gay church?*
The gay church presents the message that says, "God loves you and your behavior, too." This is simply not a Biblical position. The gay church is built on a false doctrine.

10. *Should we let homosexuals come to our church?*
How else will they get saved? And there will usually be an extended period of time (often years) during which the repentant homosexual struggles with temptation as God (through the loving relationships with other believers) meets the person's deepest needs.

11. *How can we spot the problem in our church?*
There is no surefire way. Frequently, one would run the risk of conducting a witch-hunt if he or she tried to spot people with homosexual problems in the church. It may be best to present a climate of reconciliation where a person who is struggling would feel free to come for help. In some churches the subject is never directly mentioned. That has caused some listeners to think it is so bad that it is *unmentionable,* and that can contributed to a conclusion that there is no hope for change.

12. *When is church discipline called for?*
Biblically, sin doesn't spell the end of our relationship to God or the church. David's sin with Bathsheba is a classic example. God's response included chastisement, but He did not "disfellowship" David. God's heart was for reconciliation. Many times we conclude that discipline only means punishment, but discipline also implies "teaching" and "correction." Perhaps the church needs more models of discipline and chastening that do not involve disfellowshipping. However, *known* and *unrepentant* violation does call for the three steps of Matthew 18. But only the unrepentant are disfellowshipped.

13. *How do you affirm preadolescents and adolescents in their heterosexual identity?*
Provide positive models for them. Consider having a happily married couple in every Sunday School class and youth program in the church. Let children see how God's plan for human love is worked out in a Christian context. Many of our children will not have positive models, or even a marriage model, at home.

Help erase labels. Highly creative youngsters have a strongly developed sense of independence and sensitivity. In young boys that sensitivity can cause them to feel different and rejected by male peers. Wise Christian teachers help children to see that maleness is expressed in many ways—sometimes by throwing a ball and sometimes by painting a picture or writing poetry.

Pay special attention to children from single homes where there is no same-sex parent. It is from the same-sex parent that children develop their strongest sense of conscience and responsibility. Children most easily pattern their understanding of what is right after the same-sex parent. If a father or mother is missing in the home of the children in your church, find Christians of the same sex to do extra things with these children. That same-sex adult friend can show through actions and caring what is right and what is wrong for a Christian.

Pray for the children in your church. There is no substitute for a praying faith community. As Christians, we can't totally protect our children from danger and from dangerous choices they may make. But with God's help, we can make their heterosexual identity so appealing and so wise a choice that when they are grown, they will not depart from it.

Questions Parents Ask

1. *How can I protect my son or daughter from becoming gay?*
The best way to prevent a child from becoming a homosexual is to provide a loving and caring atmosphere that provides both a mother and a father. The atmosphere ought to be one of unconditional love where the child knows that he or she can freely discuss any fears, anxieties, or problems. While this isn't a 100% guarantee, it is one of the strongest weapons against the development of a homosexual identity.

If you suspect that your child is gay, or that your child has interests, characteristics, and abilities that will make *others* think he's gay (he gets called names, etc.), it can help to have a heart-to-heart talk about peer pressures, the differences that exist, how they are not sexual, etc. A bit of practical sex education might also help.

2. *How can I tell if my son or daughter is gay?*
It is very difficult to tell if a son or daughter is gay. Most parents begin to wonder for all the wrong reasons: "He's wearing an earring." "He listens to weird music." "He doesn't date." "She doesn't seem interested in boys." Most often, the parents learn when the child tells them. Sometimes, there may be some other overt sign—discovering homosexual love letters, homosexual pornography, hearing that your son or daughter was seen near a gay hangout. Although it is painful, it is often best to wait for one of the more overt signs. When a parent comes to a child with the suspicion that he or she might be gay, it can have devastating effects if the child isn't thinking along those lines.

3. *What did I do wrong? Is it my fault?*
It is important to remember that the homosexual condition has a

variety of causes. Although you may have failed in some areas, it is likely that other circumstances played into the development of the homosexual identity. All parents have failed in some respects, and our children do have free will. They respond in many different ways.

4. *If my son or daughter is homosexual and has a lover, how should I relate to that person?*
While there are no firm rules, it may be best to handle a homosexual lover in the same way that you would handle an opposite-sex lover. Would you let your son or daughter sleep over with an opposite-sex lover? Not in a Christian context. Then you shouldn't let them sleep over in this situation either. Some parents allow the lover to come into their home for holidays and such, provided the interaction is sufficiently supervised so that further homosexual behavior is not being encouraged under their roof. In so doing, they are witnessing to the lover about the Lord, but this is delicate. It helps to realize that the lover is not the enemy, but is somebody else's son or daughter. This is a situation in which the parents should seek counseling or the prayerful advice of mature Christians.

5. *Can my son or daughter be 'fixed'?*
If he or she wants to be, God is able. But nobody can be "fixed" against his or her will.

6. *What about my own pain over this?*
You will definitely feel grief over this. Many parents go through a grief process similar to the death of a loved one—only it doesn't quit. You need support—a local ministry, a friend, Christian groups like SPATULA, "Parents in Pain," etc.

7. *Don't I have to take a stand against homosexuality?*
While you should indeed take a stand against homosexuality, you do not have to repeat that stand verbally every time you see your son or daughter. Your child will know what you think and how you feel if you've had some direct but loving communication about it. Instead of harping on the issue, use your times of interaction to minister some active love.

8. *Where can I get help?*

OVERCOMING HOMOSEXUALITY

If there is a local ministry in your area that offers counseling to homosexuals, chances are the people there would be willing to talk to you. Your pastor, if his attitudes are good, might also be an excellent resource. Nationally, there is a ministry for parents of gays called SPATULA. There are also several helpful books for parents listed in the Annotated Bibliography in the back of this book. Don't overlook sharing the dynamics between you and your child with a small group, without necessarily having to reveal the exact nature of your child's problem.

9. *How can I help my son or daughter?*
You can help best by keeping the lines of communication open. If you want your child to listen to a two-hour sermon on what's wrong with homosexuality, you might need to trade for listening to a lecture presenting his or her side. (This is especially true if your son or daughter is past the age of 18 and no longer lives at home.) If you realize that you *have* made some mistakes, you should confess them. Often this will be a catalyst which opens the door to further communication.

10. *Should I send books to my son or daughter?*
As a general rule, don't send your child any books (or sign him up for any newsletters) without his consent. If he does agree to read something, it shouldn't be lengthy. Books like *Healing for the Homosexual* and *Homosexuality: Laying the Axe to the Roots* are best. Each has less than 40 pages and mixes testimony with practical ministry.

Questions New Counselors Ask
1. *Can I really help if I don't have a homosexual past?*
Yes. In fact, in some ways you can help more than the person from a gay background. Some homosexuals change most rapidly when they are *not* working with an ex-gay counselor. It helps them to see that they are more like straight people than they thought, and that most of their problems are common to all people. These are incredibly important lessons.

2. *Is it okay for men to counsel men and women to counsel women?*
Yes, in fact it's desirable. Moberly suggests this as one healthy same-sex friendship that can lead to healing. On a practical

100

level, if you need to get down to some nitty-gritty details, it may be quite awkward to discuss them with a member of the opposite sex. (Not to imply that it isn't awkward to discuss them with a never-been-gay member of the same sex!)

3. *What do I do if my counselee falls in love with me?*
Recognize it for what it is—counterfeit backlash. Homosexual lust is a counterfeit of both heterosexual love and legitimate same-sex affections. Whenever a counselee begins moving toward either of these legitimate expressions, there will usually be feelings by association that develop because of the experience with the counterfeit. Let your client know that this is what is happening and that you can handle it.

4. *Do I have to listen to the gory details?*
Sometimes, yes. It takes awhile for a counselor to learn the distinctions. One has to hear enough to know what really happened. "I fell" isn't enough, but "I had sex with another man" might be. Sometimes it even helps to know what kind of sex the person had or wanted, but one doesn't need a minute-by-minute, sensation-by-sensation replay. One helpful clue is to realize that most clients are quite reluctant to tell *any* of the intimate details. When a client pours out all of the graphic details too quickly, one should wonder if he or she isn't getting a sexual charge out of the retelling. If this seems to be happening, but it's not certain, keep interrupting the flow of the fantasy with questions about nonsexual details: "Where did you say this happened?" "Was this someone you worked with?" "When did this happen?" "How long did you know this person?" This will pull the sexual excitement factor out of the retelling, and the client will more than likely quit.

5. *Is it okay to hug?*
Yes, but only if that's your "norm." The important thing is to treat these clients as normally as other people so that they will sense your acceptance. If your client is a new Christian or still very emotionally troubled, he or she may have an erotic reaction to a hug. This is often little more than a conditioned response.

6. *Am I in danger of getting AIDS?*
While information seems to indicate that, apart from sexual

contact or the transfusion of contaminated blood, AIDS cannot be contracted, new research is suggesting there may be ways to get AIDS in addition to direct blood contact.

7. *Can a person have a homosexual experience and enjoy it, and not be a homosexual?*
Statistics show that a large number of young adolescents have pleasurable same-sex experiences. The notion that "if you were *really* straight, then you wouldn't have enjoyed it" is false. At certain ages we can act out of curiosity about a variety of things, and many people do. And as human beings, we all can react to physical stimulation. But to think that that confirms one as gay is to believe that a much larger percentage of the population is gay than has ever been acknowledged (which some pro-gay factions might like people to believe).

8. *Are there some homosexuals who can't change?*
According to the best research, homosexuality is a learned condition and can therefore be unlearned. It is, however, a condition that may be complicated by other emotional factors that may make the process of unlearning very, very difficult. Motivation is most important. Change cannot happen without a change in attitude.

9. *How do I know when the situation is beyond me?*
It is important to realize that some issues are beyond our skills. Some people will have so many problems and such deep needs that professional help is the only direction to go. Many homosexuals also have problems beyond homosexuality. If the individual is suicidal because of severe depression and hopelessness or is talking about suicide, it is wise to get the assistance of a clinical psychologist immediately. If a client suffers from clinical depression, paranoia, or schizophrenia, referral may also be advised. Sometimes one can both refer the client and continue to work with him or her, allowing the other counselor to deal with the areas that require trained expertise.

10. *Where can I turn for help?*
Most of the ministries listed in the back of this book under "Ministry Centers" are willing to help you help others. Some offer newsletters, tapes, books, and resource lists. Some may

even be able to handle some direct questions over the phone. Make use of the books in the resource section, as well.

11. *Should I have my client get involved in a group?*
Sometimes. Groups that revolve around particular issues have both strengths and weaknesses. While groups do offer support and therapy, they may also help to foster an identity connected to the problem. For some people, a therapy group becomes an alternative to balanced Christian fellowship. When recommending a group, one should usually weigh these various factors. (Note: If an individual has some doubts about his or her sexuality, but has never identified himself or herself as gay, it is usually wise to *dis*courage involvement in a group. The group, in these circumstances, could increase the individual's homosexual identity and struggle. Sometimes it is helpful to recommend that a person go once, just to see how different he or she is from those with a deeper homosexual identity and struggle.)

12. *What about AIDS?*
Much confusion about AIDS comes from the failure to differentiate between AIDS, ARC, and "healthy carriers" with a seropositive condition.

AIDS stands for "acquired immune deficiency syndrome." The Center for Disease Control reported 26,500 confirmed cases in the United States by the fall of 1986. Of that number 15,000 had already died. AIDS victims die, not from the virus itself, but because it sabotages the body's immune system so that it's unable to fight against infection. Herpes, swollen lymph glands, perpetual diarrhea, a white fungus caked to the mouth and throat, are all symptoms. Actual death often comes from pneumonia, kidney infection, or brain infection.

ARC is "AIDS related complex." These would be diseases that are similar to AIDS and connected to AIDS but not representing a total breakdown in the body's immune system. Its symptoms may include fatigue, weight loss, fevers, chills, diarrhea, and swollen lymph glands. Some people recover from ARC and go back to being healthy carriers of the virus. Others progress into full-blown AIDS victims. It has been estimated that for every AIDS victim there are five to ten ARC cases.

Healthy carriers are the most common category. These people carry the virus lying dormant in their systems. They are said to be seropositive and have the AIDS antibody in their systems. So far only a small percentage of those who are seropositive have developed either AIDS or ARC. However, they can fatally infect other people. Also, some health care officials are becoming increasingly concerned that it may be only a matter of time before even healthy carriers develop AIDS.

13. Can I catch AIDS?
The AIDS virus can be found in any body fluid (i.e., blood, sweat, tears, semen, and urine). When the virus is transmitted into the blood, the receptive partners in anal intercourse have been the principle victims.

It has been theorized that most other sexual transmissions (i.e., homosexual oral sex and any form of straight sex) have also involved transmission into the blood via sores in the mouth or in the normally well-protected vagina. Kissing is not a recognized avenue of transmission, although some risk may exist in the presence of cold sores, fever blisters, cracked lips, or in the event of "deep" kissing.

Homosexual and bisexual men currently make up 73 percent of all AIDS victims.

Intravenous drug abusers are the next main risk group, accounting for 17 percent of the AIDS victims.

Hemophiliacs and other recipients of contaminated blood transfusions account for three percent.

Heterosexual victims are only one percent.

Uncategorized victims make up another six percent. They may actually belong to one of the other groups but are afraid to admit it.

However, noting that in Africa and Haiti AIDS appears to be striking men and women in roughly equal numbers (and is spreading to increasing numbers of heterosexuals in the United States), Robert Gallo of the National Cancer Institute in Bethesda, MD, said, "AIDS was never a homosexual virus. It's just that the homosexual group was the first to be infected in the U.S., and they spread it among themselves."

But can *you* catch AIDS? The best medical research at this point is inconclusive. It is probable you cannot catch AIDS unless (1) you have sexual contact with someone infected with the disease, (2) you are an intravenous drug user and share a needle with an infected person, or (3) you receive a transfusion of infected blood. Dr. Terri Krenshaw said it well on the CBS News Special, "AIDS Hits Home": "It won't come and get you. You've got to go out and get it."

14. *How can I best minister to those with AIDS?*
At the time of Christ, the lepers were the untouchables. The religious folks often justified their noninvolvement by suggesting that leprosy was a judgment for some hidden sin. How much easier it is for us to make a similar judgment given the direct connection between most AIDS victims and a sinful past. The response of Jesus, however, ought to be our model.

Jesus did not demand repentance before He got involved. Sometimes He responded to need. Often He responded to faith. It seems, though, that repentance was often a follow-up of sorts, as in the famous "Go and sin no more" example. Repentance is vital to salvation, but it does not seem to be a prerequisite.

Those threatened by AIDS in *any* way need the resources of Heaven. Fear, despair, and self-reproach are currently running rampant among them. Extreme, excruciating loneliness is the plight of many who are dying of AIDS. Friends often disappear out of selfishness, horror, or fear of contracting the disease themselves. Families, unable to cope with the homosexuality, the disease, or both, often disappear as well. We need to respond with compassion and concern and friendship.

Here are suggestions for specific ways to help:
1. As a pastor, you can begin by confronting attitudes of hysteria that you encounter among the homosexual's friends and family.
2. You can pray for and support efforts to find a cure for the disease.
3. You can pray that the love of God and of His people will be seen clearly in the face of this dilemma.
4. You can comfort and assist those who have been touched by the virus with "the same comfort by which we have been comforted."
5. You can lead your church in the establishment and/or support of a hospice for the victims of AIDS in your city.
6. Above all, remember that the Gospel is a message of "good news" and you are indeed a "living epistle." You need not feel pressure to quote Scriptures or present the plan of salvation on your first visit with AIDS victims. Allow them to experience your love for them, and later let them know that it was the love

of Christ that they were enjoying. This approach often provides a more lasting impact.

MINISTRY CENTER

E NGAGING IN AN EXTENDED MINISTRY TO SOMEONE WHO IS struggling with homosexuality is often more challenging than a pastor can undertake. Therefore, included is a description and means of contacting a network of ministries that clearly believes people can change from homosexual confusion. As a minister, however, you should personally contact and interview *any* specific ministry *before* referring someone to it for counseling.

EXODUS International

EXODUS International was founded in 1976 as a Christian organization dedicated to equipping and uniting agencies and individuals to effectively communicate the message of liberation from homosexuality. The organization is also dedicated to conveying support and understanding to individuals facing the reality of a homosexual loved one.

EXODUS upholds heterosexuality as God's creative intent for humanity, and subsequently views homosexual expression as outside of God's will. EXODUS cites homosexual tendencies as one of many disorders that beset fallen humanity. Choosing to resolve these tendencies through homosexual behavior, taking on a homosexual identity, and involvement in the homosexual lifestyle is considered by EXODUS to be destructive because it distorts God's intent for the individual and is therefore sinful.

Instead, Christ offers a healing alternative to those with homosexual tendencies. EXODUS upholds redemption for the homosexual person as the process whereby sin's power is broken, and the individual is freed to know and experience true identity as discovered in Christ and His church. That process entails the freedom to grow into heterosexuality. EXODUS defines this freedom as the ability to encounter the opposite sex as a needed counterpart with interest (not fear or distaste) and to relate intimately, but nonerotically, with one's own sex.

Central to this redemption is EXODUS' desire to unite and

107

equip the church to carry out this healing process. EXODUS bridges the gap between Christians who respond to homosexual men and women with ignorance and fear, and those who uphold homosexuality as a totally valid, Christ-centered life-style. To EXODUS, both extremes fail to convey to the homosexual the fullness of redemption found in Christ—He who embodies grace and truth, and invites us to partake of Him.

In order to provide individuals and agencies with a list of qualified ministries, EXODUS maintains an updated referral list. Integrity is key to the success of such ministries. As a result, EXODUS upholds specific qualifications for ministries which seek to be on its referral list, including contact with an EXODUS agency for at least six months, the director's freedom from immoral sexual behavior, agreement with EXODUS' policy and doctrine, and a governing body tied to the ministry that can remove or change its leadership.

EXODUS also endeavors to support new ministries by providing resources of experience and practical help. Such new ministries may become EXODUS affiliates if they subscribe to the organization's policy and doctrinal statement and maintain regular communication with other EXODUS agencies.

One may contact the nearest EXODUS referral agency by contacting EXODUS International, P.O. Box 2121, San Rafael, CA 94912. Phone: 1-415-454-1017.

GLOSSARY

AIDS. Acquired Immune Deficiency, a fatal disease in which the virus destroys the body's immune system leaving the body susceptible to infection. There is currently no known cure. Victims die within two to four years.

ARC. AIDS related complex, similar and connected to AIDS but not representing a total breakdown in the body's immune system. The victim may progress into an AIDS victim or recover to become a "healthy" AIDS virus carrier.

Bisexual. One who has sexual relations with either sex.

Butch. A "masculine" homosexual of either sex.

Chicken. A young male.

Chicken Hawk. An older, homosexual male who seeks young boys for sexual encounters.

Cruising. Frequenting hangouts for homosexuals with the possibility of picking up a partner. (This term is not exclusively homosexual.)

Drag. A male who impersonates a female by wearing women's attire. Also called a *Drag Queen*.

Dyke. A lesbian, usually "masculine."

EC. Evangelicals Concerned, Inc., an advocacy organization of otherwise orthodox evangelicals that attempts to justify certain homosexual behaviors—permanent marriages, etc.

EXODUS. An international association of ministries designed to help people become free from homosexual struggles. Membership is carefully restricted to established and tested ministries that agree with the association's policies and Christian doctrine.

Fairy. Derogatory slang: an effeminate, male homosexual.

Faggot. Derogatory slang: an effeminate, male homosexual.

Fem, Femme. Lesbian, usually "feminine."

Gay. Acceptable terminology describing both a member and the life-style of the homosexual community. If referring to one sex, it would be male, as in: "gays and lesbians."

Gay Bar. Hangout for the gay community. There are usually separate establishments for each sex, though the opposite sex is not excluded.

Homophobia. Irrational fear in heterosexuals of homosexuals.

Invert. Someone who was *supposedly* born a homosexual and is therefore "unable" to change. Used in contrast to "pervert."

Lesbian. Female homosexual, the accepted term.

MCC. Metropolitan Community Church, the gay church.

Pervert. Someone who was inclined to be heterosexual but *perverted* his or her inclination to become homosexual. Contrasted to "invert."

Queen. An effeminate, male homosexual.

Sodomite. A homosexual. The term is taken from the Biblical town of Sodom. If it is used in a technical sense, it could have either homosexual or heterosexual connotations and would refer to the initiator (rather than recipient) in anal intercourse.

Straight. A heterosexual.

Transsexual. A person who believes he or she is of the opposite sex.

Transvestite. One who dresses in the clothing of the opposite sex.

Trick. The person and act of picking up someone for a sexual encounter, sometimes for pay (as in prostitution).

NOTES

Chapter One

1. Robert Kronemeyer, 1980. *Overcoming Homosexuality* (Macmillan Publishing Co., Inc., 1980) p. 7.

Chapter Two

1. John R. W. Stott, "Homosexual 'Marriage,' " in *Christianity Today*, November 22, 1985, p. 25.
2. David Field, *The Homosexual Way—A Christian Option?* (InterVarsity Press, 1979), p. 19.
3. Kenneth Gangel, *The Gospel and the Gay* (Thomas Nelson, Inc., Publishers, 1978), p 56.
4. Frank Worthen, *Steps Out of Homosexuality* (Love in Action, 1984), pp. 4, 5.

Chapter Three

1. Elizabeth R. Moberly, *Homosexuality: A New Christian Ethic* (James Clarke, 1983), p. 2.
2. Ibid., pp. 5, 6.
3. Ibid., p. 3.
4. Ibid., pp. 4, 5.
5. Ibid., p. 10.
6. Ibid., p. 20.
7. Elizabeth R. Moberly, *Psychogenesis: The Early Development of Gender Identity* (Routledge and Kegan Paul, Ltd., 1983), p. 67.

Chapter Five

1. Some approach the healing of memories by having the person "image" Jesus entering the situation and changing the circumstances—such as leading a wayward father to return to the family he deserted. I am uncomfortable with this. God is all-powerful, and could enter time at any point to change history. But He seems to impose certain limits on Himself, and one of those is that He honors the free will of humans—even though it hurts. I am more comfortable with asking Jesus to reveal to the person that He was there all the time, that He cared, and that He was very saddened by the pain (which is all true). Then, I think it is more accurate to ask Jesus to *heal* the hurt that did occur, not alter the circumstances so that it didn't occur. This latter seems more true to reality and consistent with the

111

Biblical reports of the healing Jesus did while on earth.
2. Leanne Payne, *The Broken Image* (Crossway Books, 1981), p. 46.
3. New Christians or those seriously struggling with life-dominating sins may not be in a place where "ministry to others" is appropriate, but everyone is needed for service.

Chapter Seven

1. Clifford Allen, *A Textbook of Psychosexual Disorders* (Oxford University Press, 1962), p. 170.

Alcorn, Randy C. *Christians in the Wake of the Sexual Revolution: Recovering Our Sexual Sanity*. Portland: Multnomah Press, 1985. This "Critical Concern" book is a balanced approach to the various sexual problems that we face in our modern society. Dealing with topics like sex and the media, sex and the children, pornography and other sex crimes, and the homosexual movement, among others, this book chronicles the real problems without exaggeration. Besides detailing the problems, the author also provides two helpful sections entitled, "God Has Something to Say" and "What Can We Do to Promote Sexual Purity?"

Baker, Don. *Beyond Rejection: The Church, Homosexuality, and Hope*. Portland: Multnomah Press, 1985. A moving account of one church's confrontation and gradual restoration of a staff member discovered in immorality; a brief but instructive portrait of sin's consequences, church discipline and forgiveness, and the potential of repentance and healing for the individual.

Bell, Alan P., Ph.D, and Weinberg, Martin S., Ph.D. *Homosexualities: A Study of Diversities Among Men and Women*. New York: Simon and Schuster, 1978. This official publication of the Institute for Sex Research founded by Alfred C. Kinsey provides the most extensive research to date (lengthy interviews with 1,500 persons from the San Francisco bay area) on the nature of homosexual behavior. It does not, however, provide information on the etiology (the origin or cause) of homosexuality.

Bogle, Darlene. *Long Road to Love*. Washington Depot, CT: Chosen Books, 1985. This is one of the few books that chronicles a lesbian's struggles. Although it may be a bit too candid in parts, the message of hope for overcoming the lesbian struggle is clear.

Cavanagh, John R., M.D. *Counseling the Homosexual*. Huntington, IN: Our Sunday Visitor, Inc., 1977. Written from a Catholic perspective (and even dealing with homosexuality in religious orders), this well-done book is a primary reference work prepared for the working professional but clearly enough written to be helpful for the public.

Collins, Gary R. *The Rebuilding of Psychology*. Wheaton: Tyndale House Publishers, 1977. Subtitled "An Integration of Psychology and Christianity," this book details the major problems with modern psychology while holding onto those parts that are consistent with a Christian faith.

Davidson, Alex. *The Returns of Love*. Downers Grove, IL: InterVarsity Press, 1970. This book is the chronicle of one Christian man's struggles to overcome homosexuality. While it holds little hope for an "ultimate healing" of the homosexual condition, it is a vivid portrayal of the process out of emotional distress into emotional maturity.

Field, David. *The Homosexual Way: A Christian Option?* Downers Grove, IL: InterVarsity Press, 1979. A concise and penetrating analysis of what the Bible says about homosexuality presented by the senior tutor at Oak Hill Theological College in London.

Gangel, Kenneth. *The Gospel and the Gay*. Nashville: Thomas Nelson, Inc., Publishers, 1978. Long (and good) on theology, this book by the president of Miami Christian College, is a little short on theoretical understandings of the causes of homosexuality or any practical counseling suggestions for ministering to homosexuals.

Hurst, Ed. *Factors in Freedom*. Minneapolis: Factors In Freedom, 1986. (Available for $3.00 from Factors In Freedom, P.O. Box 80046, Minneapolis, MN 55408.) This booklet, subtitled, "The Struggle with Life-Dominating Sin," is designed to be a basic discipleship tool for anyone coming out of a "life-style" sin. It contains principles on understanding freedom, burning the bridges to the past, building a sure foundation, overcoming the obstacles, reckoning with the roots, and walking in freedom. Many of the concepts in *Factors in Freedom* have been included in this book.

Homosexuality: Laying the Axe to the Roots. Minneapolis: OUTPOST, 1980. (Available for $3.00 from OUTPOST, 1821 University Ave., S-296, St. Paul, MN 55104.) This booklet looks at various factors that contribute to the formation of the homosexual identity and feed current struggles. Looks at rejection, self-pity, envy, bitterness, fear, rebellion, deception, moral impurity, and oppression and their connection to homosexuality. For both pastors and those who are struggling. Many of the concepts in *Homosexuality: Laying the Axe to the Roots* have been included in this book.

Hurnard, Hannah. *Hind's Feet on High Places*. Wheaton: Tyndale, 1975. This popular allegory has been helpful in showing those struggling with homosexuality that their struggles are not unlike those of other Christians. Many identify readily with "Much-Afraid" and the entire "Fearing" family.

Inrig, Gary. *Quality Friendship*. Chicago: Moody Press, 1981. Addresses an area that most Christians struggling with homosexuality have major concerns about, the formation of "quality friendships." Detailing both the risks and the rewards of forming close friendships, this book is practical for any Christian who has difficulty forming healthy friendships.

Johnson, Barbara. *Fresh Elastic for Stretched-Out Moms*. Old Tappan, NJ: Fleming H. Revell Co., 1985. This sequel to *Where Does a Mother Go to Resign?* continues the story of the daily struggle with grief and pain when a mother discovers her son is gay.

Where Does a Mother Go to Resign? Minneapolis: Bethany House Publishers, 1979. This book is an excellent resource for hurting parents. It is written by the founder of SPATULA Ministries, and provides a humorous look at the pains and frustrations of a mother who discovers that her son is gay. It is good for parents dealing with any kind of grief and pain associated with their children.

Kronemeyer, Robert. *Overcoming Homosexuality*. New York: MacMillan Publishing Co., Inc., 1980. After a quarter century of clinical experience, Dr. Kronemeyer claims that homosexuality is a learned response to early painful experiences that can be unlearned. He uses Syntonic Therapy—"syn" for together, "tonic" for vibration or energy—to enable the gay person to relive the damaging preverbal experiences of birth and infancy. His understandings of the origins largely correspond to some Christian therapists: however, his therapy is a modified Zen approach.

LaHaye, Tim. *Spirit-Controlled Temperament*. Wheaton: Tyndale, 1966. One of the first of a new wave of books on the differences in temperaments, this book (and others like it) can help to reconcile an individual to his or her own identity. It would seem that most homosexuals have strong "melancholic" tendencies. This book explores both the strengths and weaknesses of this and other temperaments.

Lewis, C. S. *The Four Loves*. New York: Harcourt Brace Jovanovich, 1960. Lewis discusses the dangers and the rewards of close friendships exploring questions of sex, possessiveness, jealousy, pride, false sentimentality, and good and bad manners in friendships. Very useful for the Christian struggling with homosexuality but looking for appropriate friendships.

Lewis, Margie M. *The Hurting Parent*. Grand Rapids: Zondervan, 1980. An excellent resource for parents of "wayward children." The author identifies clearly with the pain, the guilt, and the frustration of Christian parents who have "failed." This book is an excellent source of comfort, resolution, and hope for the hurting parent.

Lovelace, Richard. *Homosexuality: What Christians Should Do About It*. Old Tappan, NJ: Fleming H. Revell Co., 1978. A careful analysis of the Biblical data from a conservative point of view, with a critical evaluation of the homophobic reaction of the church to homosexuals.

Lutzer, Erwin W. *How to Say No to a Stubborn Habit*. Wheaton: Victor Books, 1979. Designed both for personal use and as a group study guide, this book confronts the battle with temptation head-on. It contains chapters on renewing your mind, living with your feelings, and taming your will.

Living with Your Passions. Wheaton: Victor Books, 1983. A practical guide to sexual purity that lends itself to group study as well as personal use. It contains chapters on dealing with sexual desires and passions and the consequences and practical advice on controlling our thoughts and contending with Satan's strategies. It also contains one chapter specifically addressing homosexuality.

Moberly, Elizabeth R. *Homosexuality: A New Christian Ethic*. Cambridge, England: James Clark and Co. Ltd., 1983. (Distributed in the United States by the Attic Press, Inc., Route 2, Stoney Point, Greenwood, SC 29646.) This book represents a radical, new approach to the homosexual problem. Dr. Moberly connects the concept of "defensive detachment," the "reparative drive," and the "approach/avoidance conflict" to explain the source of homosexuality. In the author's words, this book "attempts to correlate the insights of psychology and of theology, in order to suggest what healing can mean for the homosexual and how it may be achieved." This is widely accepted among many of the ex-gay ministries as a "breakthrough" work. It is often regarded as the layman's and Christian version of her book for professionals, *Psychogenesis*.

Psychogenesis: the Early Development of Gender Identity. London and Boston: Routledge and Kegan Paul Ltd., 1983. Explores the roots of homosexual identity and offers guidelines for healing. It contains references to most of the significant studies that have been done on the homosexual issue and discusses both the strengths and weaknesses of those studies. Although written by a Christian, this book is clinical in nature and attempts to reach the psychological community.

Mumford, Bob. *The Purpose of Temptation.* Old Tappan, NJ: Fleming H. Revell Co., 1973. Many strugglers view temptation as just another chance to fail. This book takes a more positive approach to the subject and enables strugglers to see the value and the purpose for temptation in our lives.

Payne, Leanne. *The Broken Image: Restoring Personal Wholeness Through Healing Prayer.* Westchester, IL: Crossway Books, 1981. Payne's emphasis is on the restoration of a person's wholeness through healing prayers. The book is filled with hope but may underplay the often long and difficult process full healing sometimes takes.

Presbyterian Charismatic Communion. *Healing for the Homosexual.* Oklahoma City: Presbyterian Charismatic Communion, Inc., 1978. This $2.00 booklet contains various testimonies, practical steps out of homosexuality, and a pastor's guide. Good for both the pastor and the client.

Rekers, George A. *Growing Up Straight: What Every Family Should Know About Homosexuality.* Chicago: Moody Press, 1982. Highly qualified professor of child development at the University of Kansas stresses the critical role of the father in the child's psychosexual development.

Shaping Your Child's Sexual Identity. Grand Rapids: Baker Book House, 1982. Challenges the unisex philosophy and includes a firsthand report on a widely publicized court case in which a lesbian was denied custody of her children.

Seamands, David A. *Healing for Damaged Emotions.* Wheaton: Victor Books, 1981. Deals with common issues of struggle for Christians including guilt and grace, depression, low self-esteem, perfectionism, and the "wounded healer." It is good for both personal use and group study.

Putting Away Childish Things. Wheaton: Victor Books, 1982. This is an excellent tool for dealing with immature behaviors. It is designed for both personal and group use.

Smith, David W. *The Friendless American Male*. Ventura, CA: Regal Books, 1983. Many Christian males who struggle with homosexuality will admit that their strongest need is simply for a close, intimate, same-sex friend. Our society, however, has emphasized independence for males. David Smith chronicles the plight of the friendless American male and provides practical guidelines that detail not only the legitimate need for healthy same-sex friendships but also how to build those relationships.

Thorkelson, Lori. *Emotional Dependency*. (Available for $1.00 from Exodus International, P.O. Box 2121, San Rafael, CA 94912.) This small booklet deals with an issue that most individuals struggling with homosexuality face. It is a clear and concise look at the dynamics of emotional dependency, how to avoid it, and how to correct it.

White, John. *Eros Defiled: the Christian and Sexual Sin*. Downers Grove, IL: InterVarsity Press, 1977. This remains one of the most compassionate Christian books to address sexual struggles. It is an excellent resource for both the struggler and the one who counsels. Apart from two weaknesses in the section on homosexuality (too much attention to the unproved "dominant mother" theory and a shortage of hope in the "life as a nonheterosexual" section), this book is one of the most readable and helpful.

Wilkerson, David. *Two of Me: The Struggle with Sin*. Lindale, TX: Garden Valley Publishers, 1980. Planned as a booklet to lead homosexuals and others to freedom, Wilkerson claims he soon realized he was on a personal ten-year search for complete victory in his own life. His conclusion is that "no person can get his eyes on God until he gets his eyes off his own evil."

Wilson, Earl D. *Sexual Sanity: Breaking Free from Uncontrolled Habits*. Downers Grove, IL: InterVarsity Press, 1984. Explores the roots of sexual insanity, common sexual struggles (including masturbation, voyeurism, promiscuity, pornography, and homosexuality), and returning to sexual sanity.

The Undivided Self: Bringing Your Whole Life in Line with God's Will. Downers Grove, IL: InterVarsity Press, 1983. A challenge to embrace personal wholeness with an emphasis on finding a balanced life complete with emotional healing. It also contains helpful chapters on releasing forgiveness and resolving responsibility (the issue of blame).

Worthen, Frank. *Steps Out of Homosexuality.* (Available through Love In Action, P.O. Box 2655, San Rafael, CA 94912.) It is a practical guide by one of the pioneers of the ex-gay movement. Contains helpful information on the Biblical view of homosexuality, correcting our image of God, ourselves, and others, belief principles, and steps out of homosexuality.